THE BEDDGE

The Beddgelert Revival

Eryl Davies

BRYNTIRION PRESS

Published by Bryntirion Press
Bryntirion, Bridgend CF31 4DX, Wales, UK
Printed by Cambrian Printers, Aberystwyth, SY23 3TN

Contents

Foreword

Beddgelert is well known for its natural beauty; over the years people have flocked to the village to enjoy the scenery. During the period 1817–1822 many visited this beautiful area, some of them from across the border in England. They were coming, however, not to see the work of God's hand in creation, but rather to see the work of God's grace. A revival was taking place in Beddgelert, Nant and Dolwyddelan, Caernarvonshire, a revival that was to have a lasting influence on these localities and also on other areas in Wales.

A number of authors have written accounts of this Revival. Apart from a few references in Welsh biographies, these are to be found mainly in Welsh periodicals, and the one account that was published in book form is now nearly a hundred years old. There was real need to retell the story, to clarify a number of points and to present a fresh assessment. Dr Eryl Davies has succeeded admirably in accomplishing all three tasks.

In some accounts of revival there is a tendency to be too anecdotal; indeed, the fact that so many stories of interest have been preserved makes this difficult to avoid. In the account that follows, the anecdotes are set firmly in their historical context; the author considers them against the background of the latter part of the eighteenth century, and also traces their link with later revivals that are less well-known.

The story of what happened in Nant, Beddgelert and Dolwyddelan is here fully told. The origins of the awakening in each of these places are significant, for they clearly reveal the providence and grace of God. In Nant, a child was given the spirit of prayer, while at the same time the elders of the church were constrained to pray for a quickening of the Spirit. In Beddgelert, a person who had never been to the church applied for membership, and there were undoubted marks of grace in his life; members, and children, were quickened in spirit, and there was further blessing under the preaching of the Word. At Dolwyddelan God was also working among the children, and here under the preaching of the Word whole families were converted. Furthermore, we see how all three places were linked together through different individuals.

Attention is also given to particular aspects of the Revival; among these is the great emphasis given to biblical preaching. The author comments helpfully on the relationship between election and preaching. Preachers both unknown and well-known were used in this remarkable work; in addition, the Revival produced preachers of repute such as John Jones, Talsarn (who was also a musician), and Henry Rees, who became one of the main leaders of Calvinistic Methodism in the nineteenth century. A whole chapter is devoted to the 'Revival Phenomena' that occurred in a work of revival that gave a central place to preaching. To help the reader consider this matter, the author presents a number of useful points .

We are greatly indebted to Dr Davies for this thorough work of research. It is one that should encourage a serious study of other neglected revivals. Here we are given valuable insights into the nature of revival—something that is much needed in the present church situation. Furthermore, it should stimulate in the reader a prayerful concern for revival in our day.

It is a pleasure to recommend this work.

NOEL GIBBARD

Cardiff
May 2004

Preface

I am grateful to the Evangelical Library of Wales for inviting me to give its Annual Lecture in 1987. The suggested subject was the Beddgelert Revival. Dr E. Wyn James, former secretary of the Library, also encouraged me in its preparation.

It was a privilege to share much of this material in the Evangelical Movement of Wales Ministers' Conference in Bala in June 1987, and then, in August that year, to deliver the Library Lecture at the EMW Annual English Conference in Aberystwyth.

While excited and humbled by what I had read about the Beddgelert revival, I felt the need to extend my research further, and also to deal with inaccuracies in some secondary sources, including questions of chronology. Due to so many other commitments, my research over recent years has been intermittent, but I am delighted to have reached the stage when the work can be published and shared more widely.

I am indebted to the Rev. Dr Noel Gibbard of Cardiff for his kind Foreword and also for reading the manuscript in draft. His valuable suggestions have been incorporated into the text.

In addition, my thanks are due to Bryntirion Press for patiently waiting for my manuscript, and to Miss Brenda Lewis for her painstaking editing. Mrs Chris Connor has put my untidy scribble on to disk and prepared it for submission to the publisher. I am grateful to her.

Above all, I am grateful to the Lord for his sovereign grace, and for the ways in which he has quickened me through this research and given me greater longings for a divine visitation.

ERYL DAVIES

Evangelical Theological College of Wales
June 2004

Map of Wales

showing principal
places in the book

ANGLESEY
Llangefni
Rhyl
Holywell
Bangor
Denbigh
Caernarfon
Ruthin
Hafod y Llan
Bontuchel
Clynnog Fawr
Beddgelert
Llangollen
LLŶN
Porthmadog
Capel y Nant
Bala
Pwllheli
Aberdaron
Barmouth
Dolgellau
Pontrobert
Llanbryn-mair
Llanidloes
Aberystwyth
Llangeitho
Tŵr-gwyn
Tregaron
Nevern
Lampeter
Builth Wells
Llandovery
Pantycelyn
Talgarth
Llandeilo
Brecon
St Clears
Carmarthen
Llanelli
Tredegar
Swansea
Rhondda
Caerphilly
Llan-gan
Cardiff

1
Revivals in Wales

In the winter of 1816, in the Llŷn peninsula of north-west Wales, a young lame boy decided on a plan of action. His problem was that after the Sunday afternoon preaching service he had a couple of hours to wait until the commencement of the Sunday school. Feeling bored with playing with other children during this time, he hit on an effective and even ingenious plan. As soon as the afternoon congregation left the small chapel building, he hid secretly in the chapel loft. No one knew his whereabouts until, one Sunday afternoon, a girl noticed his movements and insisted on joining him. On condition that she would not be a nuisance, he allowed her to come up to the loft with him.

Almost immediately, both children began to pray together earnestly for the Lord to bless and revive the church. Gradually other children joined them, and a spirit of prayer was given to them all. Unknown to the children, the church members had also begun to pray regularly for the Lord to make the preaching and teaching of the Word powerful and effective in their church. By January 1817 there were encouraging signs that their prayers were being answered. The Lord had revived his work in the Calvinistic Methodist cause known as Capel y Nant.

Beddgelert

The story now moves from the Llŷn peninsula to Beddgelert, a large parish located about ten miles south of Caernarfon. As we shall see in later chapters, the 1817 revival is inseparably linked with both Capel y Nant and Beddgelert, at least in its beginnings and early development.

Come in your imagination to a small farmhouse in the Beddgelert area one Sunday evening in August 1817. Here there was a remarkable preaching service. The congregation had not experienced anything like it before, nor had they expected anything unusual or remarkable to happen. That was also true for the preacher, Richard Williams of Brynengan. A faithful, sincere man, he was regarded as a very ordinary preacher, and he made no pretence to being more than that.

On that August Sunday evening, however, it was different. An ordinary preacher in a routine service was given exceptional power from heaven as he began to preach. The effect on the congregation was electrifying. No one could sing the hymn after the sermon, and they all made their way home subdued and without speaking to friends or relatives. Even the preacher was stunned; he was unsure whether he had preached; it was as though he had been listening to the message himself. But Richard Williams had preached; revival was breaking out in the Beddgelert area, and it was to continue and spread extensively throughout the North for almost five years, until 1822.

Title

The revival is popularly referred to as 'The Beddgelert Revival', but this title can be misleading for at least two reasons. First, the revival commenced in Capel y Nant in Llŷn, not in Beddgelert, and this needs to be underlined. In fact, it was news of the revival in Capel y Nant that stimulated Christians in the Calvinistic Methodist church in Beddgelert to pray for the same divine blessing upon their own church. A second reason is the extent of this work. Rather than being a localised village revival, as the title suggests, it overflowed into, and powerfully affected, much of the north Wales area.

There are, nevertheless, positive arguments in favour of retaining the traditional title. One is that since many writers over the years, historians included, have used it with reference to this revival, it avoids confusion to retain the title. Secondly, the revival reached and affected the parish of Beddgelert in a major way, and in view of the many powerful as well as exciting early expressions of the revival in this parish, Beddgelert itself has over the years gained a central place in people's minds when they discuss or recall the 1817–22 revival in north Wales.

But there is a third and related argument that is even more persuasive, namely, that it was in Beddgelert, to quote Henry Hughes, that the revival 'broke out of its embankment and flooded the whole country'[1] in north Wales. And having overflowed in Beddgelert, it is a fact that the revival continued in great power within that parish, although not confined to it.

Readers may have detected my personal preference for an extended title such as 'The Revival in Capel y Nant and Beddgelert, 1817–1822'. Both factually and chronologically this would be more accurate; yet I readily acknowledge that Beddgelert soon became the epicentre of this remarkable work. For this reason I am retaining the traditional title 'The Beddgelert Revival' to refer to the powerful spiritual awakening that took place in north-west Wales and extended over a five-year period from early 1817.

National revivals

The three main dates relating to the outbreak of major and national revivals in Wales are 1735, 1859 and 1904. The Evangelical Revival of 1735 onwards was extensive in its influence in England, Wales and Scotland. In England, the leading preachers were George Whitefield[2] and John Wesley,[3] whereas in Wales God raised up Daniel Rowland[4] and Howell Harris.[5] Both Rowland and Harris were converted in 1735.

Rowland's conversion led to the transformation of his preaching ministry in Llangeitho Parish Church in Cardiganshire, west Wales. People travelled from the north and south of Wales to hear him preach the Word, and approximately two thousand would receive Holy Communion from him when the sacrament was administered. 'No British preacher of the eighteenth century', writes Bishop J. C. Ryle, 'kept together in one district such enormous congregations of souls for fifty years as Rowlands did.'[6]

Although not ordained like Rowland, Harris became an effective and famous 'exhorter'; locally at first in the Talgarth district near Brecon, and then more widely, forming converts and other concerned people into 'religious societies'. Harris's ministry was extensive and fruitful; at times he co-operated with Rowland in the work of spreading and supporting the Christian gospel. While both men visited and preached in north Wales on occasions, the impact of this revival on the North was more limited.

1859 and 1904

The next national revival in Wales after 1735 was in 1859, but in many areas there was 'no acknowledged or predominant leader',[7] although the Rev. Humphrey Jones initially and the Rev. David Morgan especially were used in this revival. It is estimated[8] that as a direct result of the 1859 Revival about 110,000 people professed faith in Christ and became members of Protestant churches in Wales; 'four-fifths' of these converts 'were reckoned among the nonconformist ranks'.[9]

The 1904 Revival tends to be referred to more frequently in Wales, partly for the reason that older Christians today still remember meeting in their younger days those blessed in that revival. During 1904–5, about 100,000 people were brought into church membership in the Principality, the Congregationalists recording the highest figure of 26,500. The Calvinistic Methodists received 24,000 new members and the Wesleyans just over

4,000. The Baptists and the Anglican churches in Wales brought the figure up to 100,000.[10]

Evan Roberts was not involved in the origin of this revival; he was part of its fruit and was used in its spread, especially in south Wales and the county of Glamorgan. In some areas, such as north Wales, the revival spread without his influence and presence, even though Roberts spent about three months there, including a time at Liverpool.

Not only was there an impact on Welsh society and on the Protestant denominations, but the revival also influenced Christians worldwide as news of it was circulated—by visitors to Wales, newspapers, magazines and, especially, Welsh missionaries. 'One of the most intriguing aspects of the Welsh Religious Revival of 1904', writes Eifion Evans, 'is its global spread. Within a comparatively short time of its commencement people were flocking to this little-known country of the Celtic fringe of Europe from neighbouring countries and across oceans.' He adds: 'A decade later and all five continents had experienced its influence.'[11]

In what is an invaluable and stimulating book, *On the Wings of the Dove*,[12] Noel Gibbard ably traces the international impact of the 1904–5 Welsh revival: on Europe (countries like Holland, France, Germany, Scandinavia and Russia), the Americas and the West Indies, Africa and Madagascar, Asia, then Australia and New Zealand. This is an exciting read.

Local revivals

In their ignorance, some Christians assume that little of spiritual significance occurred in Wales between 1735 and 1859, or between 1859 and 1904; they also tend to assume that no other revivals were experienced in Wales between 1735 and 1904. The real facts, however, are very different indeed.

Daniel Rowland, who died in 1790, preached continuously for years in revival in west Wales. But independent of Rowland and

Harris, even during the 1760s, 1770s and 1780s, small local revivals broke out in different areas of Wales: from Rhymney in Gwent to Aberffraw in Anglesey, Llanbryn-mair in mid-Wales to Clynnog and also Brynengan in north-west Wales, Crug-y-bar in Carmarthenshire to Bala in Merioneth. For example, in 1781 a powerful local revival broke out in Crug-y-bar under the ministry of Isaac Price, the Congregational pastor. Nearly all of Price's ministry was undertaken in revival or as a result of revival, and many churches were blessed under his preaching.

During the 1790s, a number of local revivals were experienced in Bala in connection with the new Sunday school work there and the preaching of Thomas Charles.[13] 'Here in Bala', wrote Charles in 1791, 'we have been blessed with a great, powerful and glorious outpouring of the Spirit on the people, especially on the children and young people. Scores of wild and indifferent young people have been awakened . . .'[14]

Between 1805 and 1862
Another local revival occurred in Aberystwyth in 1805, affecting many children and adults,[15] and there were more local revivals in 1811 linked with Sunday schools in different areas. A church prayer meeting in Bontuchel in Denbighshire during 1821 ended in revival; the preaching of the Word became irresistible, resulting in many powerful conversions of worldly people living in the vicinity. Other local revivals followed—in Anglesey (1822), Carmarthen (1828), Pwllheli (1831), Caernarfon (1832), Merioneth, Liverpool and areas of south Wales (1840). In Merioneth alone, 'above two thousand souls were added to one denomination'.[16]

The reappearance of the dreaded cholera epidemic in some parts of south Wales in 1849 encouraged many to consider the claims of the Christian gospel. Thomas Rees reported in May 1850[17] that the period from the end of 1843 to the summer of

1849 'was a season of almost universal spiritual declension, but last year [1849] most of the churches in the counties of Monmouth and Glamorgan, and many in those of Brecon and Carmarthen, were blessed with a most powerful revival'. Rees estimates that between 1200 and 1500 persons were added to the nine Congregational churches in the Merthyr area, and at least 1000 to the Carmarthenshire churches, in addition to those in places like Llandovery, Llangadog, Llandeilo, Carmarthen and Llanelli.[18] One thing he emphasises is that the revival was not confined to his own Congregational denomination: 'Some thousands were added to the Baptist churches in the counties of Monmouth and Glamorgan,' he adds, 'and great numbers joined the Calvinistic and Wesleyan Methodist Societies in some localities.'

Further local revivals took place in Henllan in Cardiganshire (1850) and in Staylittle, Montgomeryshire (1851), the latter connected with a series of prayer meetings held in a local church. The claim made by Eifion Evans that between 1762 and 1862 'there were at least fifteen outstanding revivals in Wales'[19] is justified; but note that he is referring not to the total number of revivals, but rather to those revivals that were 'outstanding' in terms of their power and influence.

Between 1859 and 1904

Even between 1859–60 and 1904 there were further examples of local and regional revivals. During 1866, for example, many denominations reported extensive blessing, as in Tredegar and Port Talbot, while in 1871 numerous churches in south-east Wales, the Rhondda valleys and along the southern coastline witnessed hundreds of professions of faith in their localities.

In 1887 it was the turn of Carmarthenshire, especially the Baptists, then that of the Independents in Blaenau Ffestiniog in the North, to experience revival. In the north Wales area, Richard Owen, the Welsh Presbyterian evangelist, was greatly used, particularly in the early 1880s. Late in 1890, in response to daily covenanted prayer by the church for conversions, the Lord visited Caersalem Chapel, Dowlais, in power; and in 1892, again in response to fervent prayer, the Baptist church in Pontnewydd, Monmouthshire.

I have illustrated the point extensively in order to emphasise that between the major revivals of 1735, 1859 and 1904, Wales has also been privileged to experience many local and regional revivals. There is, therefore, considerable evidence in favour of calling Wales 'the land of revivals'. And it is in this pattern of regional revivals that we need to place the 1817–22 revival at Capel y Nant and Beddgelert.

'. . . this great revival . . . '

That is how William Williams,[20] in 1871, described the 1817–22 revival in north-west Wales, as he detailed, over six pages, the main events relating to the revival at Beddgelert. Edward Griffiths[21] uses similar language, calling it 'a great and blessed awakening'. Edward Thomas[22] agrees: 'We received another powerful outpouring of the Spirit when the Beddgelert revival broke out in the year 1817. We have not had as powerful a revival as this before in the North.' Another historian[23] concludes that the revival's 'influence was deep, especially on the County of Caernarfon'. Contemporary historians agree with this positive assessment. For example, D. Gareth Evans refers to 'a most powerful revival, the awakening that started at Beddgelert in Caernarvonshire from 1817 to 1822'.[24] Similarly, Eifion Evans describes it as 'a remarkable spiritual awakening', adding, 'It was one of the most powerful revivals seen in Wales . . .'[25] Gomer Roberts, a competent church historian on this period in Wales, describes the Beddgelert revival as 'that great revival'.[26]

Dr R. Tudur Jones focuses on the Beddgelert revival when considering briefly the influence of religious revivals on Wales.

He reminds us that revivals have varied

> in terms of their nature, their geographical spread and their passion. Some revivals reached the whole of Wales, like the 1859–60 revival. Others were restricted to areas, like the 1849 revival in Glamorgan. Some revivals are heavy in their influence but without any great excitement, while others were extremely exciting in their effect.[27]

The influence of the 1817–22 revival, according to Tudur Jones, was considerable in terms of evangelism, church planting, and the numbers of young men converted and then called to the preaching ministry, some of whom, like John Jones, Tal-sarn, and Cadwaladr Owen, became effective preachers. There was also a cultural, moral and social impact. For example, Tudur Jones concurs with the suggestion of Henry Hughes that the Beddgelert revival stimulated a Welsh literary/cultural awakening and inspired the patriotic formation, around 1822, of some of the eisteddfods and Welsh societies.[28]

The origins, development and influence of this 1817–22 revival will be described and assessed in later chapters, but I am underlining here the widely acknowledged fact that, among all the local regional revivals in nineteenth-century Wales, the Beddgelert revival stands out in terms of its importance and influence. Griffith Owen, the biographer of Cadwaladr Owen, does not exaggerate when he claims, 'The Beddgelert revival deserves special attention, as an important historical period for religion in our country.'[29] Chapters two to four will provide the national and local background to this revival.

2
Life in Wales, social and religious

B efore describing in detail the beginnings and development of the revival in Capel y Nant and Beddgelert in north-west Wales, it is necessary first to describe briefly the social, economic and religious conditions prevailing in Wales early in the nineteenth century.

Population
In 1770, the population of Wales was approximately 500,000;[1] but by 1851 this had more than doubled to 1,163,000. When the first census was taken in 1801, the number of people living in Wales had risen to 587,000. By 1811 that figure had increased to 673,000;[2] this 'remarkable increase' was due to natural causes rather than to immigration.[3] In 1770 nearly all the people in Wales worked on the land, whereas in 1851 only one-third of the people worked in agriculture.[4] This represented a major change.

Crisis
The early years of the nineteenth century were years of crisis for many people in Wales. One major contributory factor was the weather. Between 1789 and 1802 there were numerous wet summers followed by disappointing harvests, bringing considerable hardship and distress to families. But the inclement weather continued well beyond 1802. For example, the winter of 1814 was exceptionally cold, while 1816 was described as 'the year without a summer' because of the constant rain and low temperatures. In

1817, famine conditions prevailed in many parts of Wales, only to be followed by powerful storms and extensive flooding, which in some areas rendered many families homeless and hungry. Because of the scarcity of food and the high prices, occasional riots broke out. From 1815 the prices of livestock fell sharply, giving farmers little option but to sell their animals in large numbers in order to obtain income for rent and for the necessities of life. Poverty became more extensive; children were often deprived, while the sick and elderly suffered as inevitable and helpless victims in the situation.

Industrialisation

Industrialisation made a quick impact on Wales, especially in the South as the nineteenth century proceeded. By 1802 the north Wales slate quarry in Bethesda was consolidated and made more efficient, to be followed later by the Dinorwic quarry in Llanberis. The Ffestiniog slate quarries were bought by a group of Lancashire men early in the century. Their business enterprise was justified, largely because demand for slate in the building industry increased extensively after 1815; indeed, demand at times outstripped supply.

In north Wales, copper mining was on the decline. By 1815 only 600 miners were employed, although in Caernarvonshire the annual copper production was 8,000 tons even in 1860, after which there was a major reduction in output and demand.

War

During the eighteenth century there had been several expensive and lengthy wars between England and France. These climaxed in the famous battle of Waterloo in 1815, thus ending the period of the French Revolutionary War (1793–1802) and the Napoleonic war between 1803 and 1815. At Waterloo, the Duke of Wellington's forces achieved 'complete victory'.[5] This was really the war which ended wars, because after 1815 France and Britain were destined never again to engage in military conflict with one another.

The French Revolution and war also had an indirect effect upon Nonconformist churches in Wales, especially the Calvinistic Methodists. To appreciate this, it is helpful to refer to the 1689 Act of Toleration which followed in the wake of the Revolution in England a year earlier.

Dissenters

On condition that ministers and members affirmed an oath of allegiance to William and Mary, rejected the Pope's jurisdiction and distinctive Roman doctrines, and also subscribed to the doctrinal sections of the Thirty-nine Articles, the 1689 Act allowed Dissenting ministers and groups of a Protestant Trinitarian position to hold religious meetings outside the State parish churches and in their own meeting houses. Such buildings had to be officially registered. This law was a relief and encouragement to the Baptists and Independents.

Further encouragement was given in 1767, when the House of Lords ruled that it was no longer a crime to be a member of, or to worship in, a Nonconformist church. In 1779 Parliament amended the Toleration Act, releasing Nonconformists from the obligation to accept the doctrinal parts of the Thirty-nine Articles when taking the Oath of Allegiance.

But the position of the Calvinistic Methodists was more ambivalent. They were not strictly Dissenters because they still officially remained as a group within the State Church. The problem was that in order to cope with the growth of the movement, they worshipped in houses or chapels, and these tended to be unlicensed. In ordinary circumstances, tolerance may have prevailed, but A. H. Dodd correctly points out that 'the panic caused by the French Revolution made all abnormal assemblies suspect and open to visitations by disorderly mobs or officers of the law'.[6] Towards the end of the eighteenth century, therefore, and on the advice of leaders like Thomas Charles, the Calvinistic Methodists began registering their meeting places to meet the requirements of the 1689 Act.[7] This was a significant 'first step'[8] or even 'half the way in forming a separate denomination'.[9] It was in 1811 that the final step was taken, with the ordination of some of their own preachers.

Sunday schools

'Educational Destitution' is how official reports describe educational facilities in Wales during the first half of the nineteenth century. Apart from a few grammar and private schools, as well as a growing number of Sunday schools, educational provision for Wales was grossly inadequate.

The circulating schools of Griffith Jones had made an important contribution earlier in the eighteenth century, and their influence continued at least until the death of Madam Bevan in 1779. By the late 1780s the formation of Sunday schools gathered momentum and slowly replaced the circulating day schools.[10] By 1789, places in north Wales as far afield as Bala, Denbigh, Holywell, Caernarfon and Llanfyllin each had a Sunday school. This work was given enthusiastic support and leadership by Thomas Charles from his Bala home. Charles also liaised with leaders of the Sunday school movement in England. The latter reported that by 1812 it had assisted 256 schools of all denominations in north Wales and 186 in south Wales.[11] In the early and later decades of the nineteenth century, the development of Sunday schools was extensive and they became an inevitable feature, and valuable instrument, of Nonconformist churches throughout the Principality.

There was considerable blessing on this Sunday school work in Wales, with some powerful revivals breaking out amongst the children. In 1804–5, for example, there was a 'children's revival' in Aberystwyth. Thomas Charles reports on what he saw there at the time:

At Aberystwyth and in the adjacent parts, there are general and powerful awakenings among the young people and children. Some hundreds have joined the religious societies in those parts. I was there lately at an Association of Calvinistic Methodists . . . The concourse of people assembled on the occasion was computed to amount at least to 20,000 . . . Hundreds of children from eight years old and upwards might be seen in the congregation, hearing the Word with all the attention of the most devout Christian, and bathed in tears.[12]

Similarly, in Caernarfon town, seven Calvinistic Methodist Sunday schools met together on Sunday 19 November 1808 for catechising and exhortation. Over the previous months they had been thoroughly grounded in such doctrines as the existence of God, the divine attributes, man in sin, new birth, redemption, heaven and hell. The Rev. John Roberts, Llangwm, reported, 'I never saw such outpourings on old people and children since many years.'[13]

But Aberystwyth and Caernarfon are only two examples of revivals which occurred within the Sunday schools of Wales during this early period of the nineteenth century. This remarkable blessing on the work made the Sunday school movement, together with Nonconformity, potent forces for positive change and development within all areas of Welsh society.

Religious life in Wales
We can now describe the more general religious situation which prevailed in the country at the time of the revival in Capel y Nant and Beddgelert in 1817.

The powerful revival which broke out in 1735 in south and mid-west Wales under Howell Harris and Daniel Rowland did not impact north Wales. While these and other men itinerated on occasions in north Wales, the blessing on their ministries there was limited and localised. The new Calvinistic Methodist movement spread extensively in the counties in mid-Wales and south Wales, and by 1780 it was firmly established. In the North, however, the situation was discouragingly different. This was due largely to 'the strength of the Established Church and widespread hostility to enthusiasm'.[14] Only a small number of congregations existed under the care of the Methodists for the preaching of the Word and the nurturing of converts. By 1750, 428 Calvinistic Methodist societies had been established, mainly in the six counties of south Wales, but only about ten congregations existed in north Wales.[15] These societies supplemented worship in Anglican churches by providing people with fellowship, exhortation, teaching and encouragement.[16]

Evangelical preaching

How much evangelical preaching was there in Wales at the end of the eighteenth century? A. H. Williams reports there were not many Wesleyans here, and fewer still of the Lady Huntingdon churches. It was doubtful, too, whether George Whitefield had more than one church to his name. However, according to Williams, there were in the Anglican Church in Wales sixty-two evangelical priests from the early period who were leaders in Calvinistic Methodism, or in touch or sympathy with it. Examples include David Jones (Llan-gan), David Griffiths (Nevern), Simon Lloyd (Bala) and William Lloyd (Caernarfon).[17] About twenty-three of these men died before the close of the eighteenth century.[18]

The year 1784 marked a significant turning point, when the Rev. Thomas Charles settled in the small town of Bala. Within a brief time, Bala became the hub of Calvinistic Methodism in north Wales. The town witnessed a number of local revivals, and occasions of outstanding and effective preaching in the Methodist Associations that met in the town annually for many years. From the lakeside town of Bala, Thomas Charles made preaching trips which proved effective and fruitful in reaching many areas in north Wales.

The Dissenting[19] churches consisted mainly of Independents (or Congregationalists) and Baptists, as well as Unitarians. R. T. Jenkins reminds us that by 1816 the Congregationalists had 267 churches in Wales.[20] A significant factor in the increase of Congregational churches was the entry of several gifted young men into the Christian ministry at the close of the eighteenth century. Despite this gradual growth, Thomas Rees correctly acknowledges that 'our denomination was very feeble and scarcely known in most parts of north Wales'[21] until the early part of the nineteenth century. Men like Dr George Lewis (Llanuwchllyn), John Roberts (Llanbryn-mair), David Morgan (Llanfyllin), Williams of Wern and others, preached effectively, with the result that weak established churches were gradually given a new lease of life and some new churches were planted.

For the Baptists, who had a mission to the North beginning in 1776, the situation was even weaker. In 1790 there were only forty-eight Baptist churches in Wales. However, within twenty years there were 176. This figure[22] includes eight Scottish Baptist[23] churches which were Sandemanian[24] in theology, as well as fifteen General Baptist[25] churches which were either Arminian[26] or even Unitarian[27] in their beliefs.

Dissenting church growth
There were reasons for the growth in the number of Dissenting churches in Wales. One important fact was that both Congregationalists and Baptists benefited spiritually from the Calvinistic Methodists, in terms of their zeal, experiences of God, teaching, and also revivals. Another reason for the increase

in the Baptist cause was the preaching ministry of men like Christmas Evans.[28]

Influenced profoundly by, and converted through, a local revival in his home area in west Wales during 1784–5, Christmas Evans joined the Baptist church in Llanybydder. A period of revival in the church occurred at this time, but in 1789 Evans went to pastor a Baptist church in the remote area of Llŷn in north-west Wales. This was the only Baptist church in the area, but there were about sixty-seven people in membership. His ministry in the Llŷn was blessed with converts, who became attached to Baptist or Methodist societies in the area.

Other parts of the country were also blessed by Evans's ministry. For example, in 1791 he embarked on a preaching itinerary along the west coast of Wales from the North down to Llanelli in the South. As a result of his ministry, multitudes of people professed faith in Christ and joined churches or 'societies' in their home areas. Also in 1791, Christmas Evans agreed to pastor the small, discouraged Baptist causes in Anglesey. This was the beginning of his thirty-four years of ministry in Anglesey, in which he was the instrument of bringing many people to Christ and also planting several Baptist churches. After two brief pastorates in south Wales, in Caerphilly and Cardiff, Christmas Evans returned north, but this time to Caernarfon and, after another useful but brief period of ministry, died in 1838.[29]

Calvinistic Methodism

What about the Calvinistic Methodists? Certainly by 1816 they formed the strongest denomination in Wales, with 343 churches.[30] Strictly speaking, as we have indicated, the Calvinistic Methodists had been disinclined to view themselves as 'Dissenters', one reason being that since the mid-1730s they had remained within the Anglican church, while arranging fellowship or 'society' meetings under their own auspices during the week in order to nurture the spiritual life of their people. By contrast, the Dissenting churches had made it a deliberate policy to establish a fellowship and chapel building as a 'substitute'[31] for the parish church rather than an 'adjunct' to it. A further reason for distinguishing themselves from Dissenters was the fact that they had enjoyed considerable blessing as a movement, and wave after wave of local and regional revivals.

Circumstances, however, made it necessary for them to form a distinct denomination. As already mentioned, the tension and fear aroused by the French Revolution and the Anglo-French war made unregistered meetings and buildings like those of the Calvinistic Methodists liable to misunderstanding, closure, and even attacks by unruly groups of local people. So, near the end of the eighteenth century and on the advice of Thomas Charles, the Calvinistic Methodists began to register their meeting places. This was an important initial step towards becoming a Dissenting denomination. The climax came in 1811 when, on account of the phenomenal growth of the work and the need for ordained leaders, a number of men were ordained to the ministry of the new Calvinistic Methodist denomination in Wales.

Phenomenal growth

Several significant factors contributed to the success of Calvinistic Methodism. One of these was the nominalism within the Established Church, coupled with the low standards of the clergy in terms of morality, spirituality, pastoral care and preaching.

Another factor was the indigenous nature of the new movement and its Welshness. In contrast, the Established Church was perceived as being more English. For example, not one Welsh-speaking bishop was appointed to a diocese in Wales between 1727 and 1870, a period of 150 years![32]

But there were other and more powerful factors that ensured the phenomenal growth of Calvinistic Methodism. For example,

Edward Thomas provides eight major reasons for its success in Wales:

the itinerant ministry of the early preachers; detailed care of their churches and societies; the use of godly and gifted lay people; the concern for doctrinal purity; the Sunday school; discerning and applying themselves to the time in which they lived; simple efforts of individuals to make the gospel known and, finally but importantly, powerful and frequent out-pourings of the Holy Spirit.[33]

'When the Holy Spirit was poured out on Wales at the time of the Methodist revival,' writes Edward Thomas, 'the denomination was born.'[34] Several other powerful revivals were to follow, like the one in 1762, and the revival in Llangeitho when Rowland was put out of the parish church. Thomas also singles out for special mention the revivals in Bala under Thomas Charles in 1791, then Beddgelert in 1817, and Pwllheli in 1832. By 1895, the Calvinistic Methodists could claim that they had 2,744 chapels, over 145,000 members, 306,000 hearers and a total annual collection of £317,000.[35]

What needs to be emphasised is that, until about 1850, there was a 'universal consensus'[36] about theology amongst the Nonconformist denominations, a consensus that was essentially evangelical and moderate Calvinism. There was 'a united front', even with the Arminian Wesleyan Methodists who gradually emerged in Wales, concerning the gospel as the central and uniting message of the major Nonconformist denominations. By contrast, the Roman Catholic population in Wales early in the nineteenth century consisted of approximately 1,000 families and eight mission centres.

It is time, in the next chapter, to outline the early developments in the two Calvinistic churches in Capel y Nant and Beddgelert, where revival broke out in 1817.

3
Beddgelert:
preparing the way

That a revival should have broken out in the locality of Beddgelert in north-west Wales was in itself unexpected and stunning. After all, the Beddgelert area was notorious for its worldliness, immorality, drunkenness and indifference to religion. Henry Hughes quotes a Mrs Elin Williams who was in school in Beddgelert before the 1817 revival commenced, and she described the area as 'a terrible, ungodly place'. Each week, Mrs Williams reported, there would be at least one night of drinking, cursing, swearing and fighting in one of the taverns.[1] In order to appreciate the situation prior to the outbreak of revival in 1817, we need to retrace our steps and outline the way in which the gospel was established in the locality.

The gospel was not preached regularly in the parish of Beddgelert until 1771.[2] Before this date, those eager to hear the Word preached had to walk twelve miles to Brynengan, which was the centre of Calvinistic Methodism for the large and scattered area of Eifionydd.

The conversion of the first Methodist in the Brynengan area probably occurred in 1751.[3] Henry Hughes states that the church was established by 1755, and a building erected in 1777.[4] Before it was completed, the building was consecrated on the occasion of Daniel Rowland ministering the Word there during his last visit to Gwynedd. The building was also used as a school.

The Methodist preacher Robert Dafydd (1747–1834) was based here. A powerful revival occurred in Brynengan in 1785, resulting in many conversions, the quickening of believers, and great rejoicing in each meeting. It was a revival that affected Llŷn and Eifionydd.

Robert Roberts of Clynnog (1762–1802) was greatly blessed through it and given an intense love for Christ as well as zeal for the conversion of people. At the time of the 1785 revival he started preaching.[5] He was a schoolmaster in the area, until gradually the work of teaching in addition to preaching became a great strain for him. At this point the Arfon Monthly Meeting advised him to give himself entirely to the preaching of the gospel. The opportunity came for him to live in the Chapel House in Clynnog Fawr and care for the church there. He stayed here until his death and was known as Robert Roberts, Clynnog, an outstanding preacher.[6]

A powerful revival occurred in Brynengan and the surrounding area in 1809; then another glorious revival broke out there in 1832, the latter being again inseparably linked with the old preacher Robert Dafydd. Aged eighty-two, he prayed perseveringly over a period of two years that the Lord would allow him to see another revival before he died. His prayers were answered in a remarkable way.

Beddgelert

However, while there was good preaching in Brynengan, and blessing upon the Word, in the Beddgelert area there was great spiritual darkness and need. But the Lord had not forgotten this locality. One example of his kindness was the school which Robert Jones, Rhos-lan, commenced in the parish church in Beddgelert about 1764.[7]

As a Christian young man, Robert Jones was eager to help others by becoming a teacher in one of the circulating schools.[8] After early rejections he was finally accepted on condition that he held a school in Beddgelert. He agreed, and his main task was to teach the children to read the Bible and explain to them the main doctrines and principles of the Christian faith. What struck Robert Jones was the extensive ignorance of the Bible in the parish. Although his life was exemplary, many of the local people objected to him teaching the Bible to the younger generation and openly opposed him.

His work as a teacher in Beddgelert was brief, but fruitful despite the opposition. We know that two people were profoundly influenced through him and became useful servants of the Lord. One of these was Robert Dafydd, later of Brynengan, whose heart was opened at the time the Word was sown in the Beddgelert school. Another person who was changed spiritually in this early period was Owen Tomos, who later moved to Anglesey and laboured there faithfully for the gospel over many years.

Concerning Beddgelert, Robert Jones reports that before the 1817 revival one could say of this area, 'Here is Zion, but no one seeks her.' The local people were so indifferent to Christianity that Jones described them as 'the people that sat in darkness'[9] and the period as a 'night of discouragement'. He spoke of the area as a wilderness (*anialwch*) and a dry, barren land (*sychtir*).[10] For about seventeen years after Robert Jones left, there was no teacher in Beddgelert and, consequently, no one to continue sowing the Word there.

Henry Thomas

Mercifully, in about 1782–3, one of the young men in the parish was converted. His name was Henry Thomas. His father was eager for him to enter the Anglican ministry, so Henry was sent to Botwnnog grammar school, some miles away in the Llŷn peninsula. It was on hearing the gospel here that Henry Thomas was converted. The new convert had such an awareness of the spiritual needs of people in Wales without Christ that, to his father's disappointment, he found it impossible to continue studying in the grammar school. On returning home to the Beddgelert area, Henry Thomas suffered considerable ridicule and opposition from local people, but he persevered in the faith and opened a daily school with the aim of teaching neighbours to read the Bible.

While opposition continued, a local man by the name of Owen Owen gave him the use of an old building called 'Yr Hen Odyn' (The Old Kiln) for his school. It was actually a small cowshed, but many local children and young people, and some adults too, came there to learn to read the Bible and to be catechised. Some prayer meetings were held, and a significant number of the younger pupils were affected savingly through reading the Word and praying together to the Lord. More of the older people wanted to be taught and they, too, came under the powerful influences of the Word. 'Soon', we are informed by one early source, 'the Lord visited this small group.'[11] Among the converts was a young lady who allowed her home to be used by visiting preachers for meetings, and another who succeeded Henry Thomas as schoolteacher.

The meetings were relocated several times on account of complaints, and also because of increased numbers attending. More formal church meetings were now held, and preachers like Robert Jones, Rhos-lan, and Gruffydd Jones, Ty'n-llech, were invited to minister the Word. Their visits were fruitful, and even unusual and exciting.

Preaching at Nanmor

Robert Dafydd, who had moved to Brynengan about 1773,[12] was concerned for the Beddgelert area, so he arranged to preach the Word to his former neighbours. It seems that Tŷ Rhisgl, a house in the area of the parish known as Nanmor, was chosen for the meeting. But because of his circumstances at the time, Robert Dafydd found himself unable to preach, so he sent Robert Jones in his place.[13]

Many locals were eager to attend the meeting, but during the sermon they were rude and inattentive. While the women knitted, the men laughed at the preacher, and he did not know how to regain order and quietness. Unexpectedly, there was a flash of lightning followed almost immediately by a frightening clap of thunder, with the result that many in the congregation were seized with fear. After a brief period of tense silence, Robert Jones began to underline the warnings of Scripture concerning God's holy judgement of sinners and their eternal destiny in hell. Several in the congregation were converted[14] and joined the small group of believers in the Nanmor area of the parish.

Only a few weeks later, the elderly Gruffydd Jones was preaching there. This time two young men from a neighbouring area were intent on disturbing the service and embarrassing the preacher. They hid in the loft of the room where the service was held and made small holes in the ceiling immediately over the pulpit. As Gruffydd Jones proceeded to preach, they pushed soil and rubble down through the small holes in the ceiling on to the open Bible in the pulpit. The preacher carefully removed the soil and dust from the Bible each time they fell but continued preaching. When the young men had used up all their soil and rubble they had no choice but to listen to the preacher. Within minutes they were listening attentively to the message and came under deep conviction of sin. At the end of the sermon they came down from their hiding place, shouting out, 'What must we do to be saved?' They were soundly converted and became active workers for the Lord in the area.

Divine protection

A preacher who ministered the Word to believers here on a later occasion was the Rev. Evan Richardson of Caernarfon. The persecution of believers continued over several years, and Evan Richardson experienced it from a local man who was actively opposed to the gospel and hated the Christians, calling them 'Roundheads'. This man used all kinds of ploys to hinder and even stop the services being held in the small church. Sometimes he wore an unusual cloak and shouted or howled as he lay on the small wooden bridge spanning the river Colwyn close to the church. On other occasions he collected stones from the river bank and threw them at the church windows from a distance of twenty feet. But he never once succeeded in breaking a window. The people who attended the services would regularly have mud and manure thrown at them, but they were never hit by the stones.

One Sunday morning Evan Richardson was preaching from near the church door, when this man approached the wooden bridge over the river with a pitchfork in hand and threatened to use it on the preacher. The man was filled with rage and intent on attacking him, but as he walked on to the bridge he found himself unable to proceed and began to tremble. After a short while, he attempted to cross the bridge again, but the trembling returned and he was forced to retrace his steps. A third time he tried to go across the bridge to the preacher but, failing again, he was seized with fear and physical trembling. Slowly, the man retreated from the scene and the preacher was enabled to complete his powerful message. The small group of believers was greatly encouraged and strengthened by this example of the Lord's protection.

Other influences

Gradually, other influences and groups came to the parish. One was a Roman Catholic Order of Mary, but their influence was limited. Another group appeared, teaching that born-again believers do not sin and placing an emphasis on singing in their services; but they stayed in the area only for a brief period. About this time, some Moravian Christians came to part of the parish, and their influence was positive. One notable convert to the Moravians was

William Gruffydd. He challenged the rising tide of ungodliness and became instrumental in the conversion of some local people. When Gruffydd moved away from the area, the Moravians who remained joined the Calvinistic Methodist fellowship.

A church building

The Calvinistic Methodists urgently needed a church building of their own, in order to avoid dependence on local landowners. In the providence of God one of the local gentry, Sir Robert Williams, Plas y Nant, agreed to a request to lease some land in the village, on which a small church could be built.

Instrumental in this development was William Williams of Ffridd, who was approached by Sir Robert Williams for his vote in the parliamentary election. Sir Robert was contesting the County of Caernarfon seat in Parliament with Lord Bulkeley. When Sir Robert asked William Williams for his personal vote, the latter agreed, but on condition that Sir Robert would lease some land in the village for them to build a Calvinistic Methodist church. Permission was given without hesitation, on condition that the believers act on the promise made by Sir Robert and proceed to erect the building immediately. Although it was small, basic and damp, the new church building[15] was appreciated by the believers and regular meetings with visiting preachers were arranged.

Glimmers in the darkness

During the years that followed, leading up to the 1817 revival, there was increased drinking of alcohol in the parish, with the accompanying drunkenness, rioting, fighting and immorality. Salaries had improved as the lead and copper mines prospered. People moved into the area because of employment prospects, some coming from England and others from Ireland and Scotland. These and other social changes encouraged greater indifference to religion and contributed further to the increasing ungodliness in society.

Despite the difficulties confronting Christians and the small Calvinistic church in the area, there were a few glimmers of hope and indications that the Lord could transform the situation. One such indication was the arrival of a group of Wesleyan Methodist preachers during the opening decade of the nineteenth century. They held services in Tŷ Mawr, Nanmor and Cwm Cloch in Nant Colwyn, and their preaching was powerful and effective. Local people were challenged and startled by their message and zeal.

Unfortunately, these Wesleyan preachers tended on occasions to be unwise in what they said about the Calvinistic Methodists, and this gave rise to tensions between the two groups as well as unloving attitudes. Within a brief period the Wesleyan work waned in its influence, and while the Calvinistic church maintained its number of members at around forty for twenty years prior to 1817,[16] the cause was ineffective and weak. Revival was desperately needed.

4
Capel y Nant:
sowing the seed

The background to the establishment of the Calvinistic Methodist church in Capel y Nant is an interesting one. It illustrates the importance of sowing the Word of God faithfully over many years, and then praying fervently to the Lord for that Word to yield a rich harvest.

In studying the early history of Calvinistic Methodism in north-west Wales, historians have tended to concentrate on the area of Llŷn or Eifionydd rather than on Arfon in the northern area of Gwynedd.[1] Howell Harris in his *Diary*, for example, Robert Jones, Rhos-lan, in his *Drych yr Amseroedd,* and others too, have given us more historical data relating to Llŷn than to the Arfon area of Gwynedd, the old Caernarvonshire.

Llŷn

The Llŷn peninsula embraced Calvinistic Methodism almost fifty years before the northern area of the county did so, and there are reasons for this. One important reason was political. During the seventeenth century, in one area of Llŷn—including Castell-march, Rhydolion, Nanhoron (which is close to Capel y Nant) and Madrun—there was strong Republican conviction. Inhabitants like Gruffydd Jones, Sieffre Parri, Rhisiart Edwards and Thomas Madrun were anti-royalists, and they were also opposed to the Established Anglican Church.[2] These men, too, played a significant part in the main political and religious issues of those days. Consequently, in this area of north-west Wales there was more sympathy on the part of the gentry towards Nonconformity.

A second reason for the early progress of Calvinistic Methodism in the Llŷn area was the continuing influence of Puritanism in the southern part of Caernarvonshire, including Llŷn. Despite the considerable persecution under Elizabeth, Charles II and James II, Nonconformity was not eradicated. It found expression, for example, in the Congregational church in Pwllheli with its various branches.

The spiritual darkness in the area as a whole, however, was extensive. Very few people were literate; in addition, the shortage of Welsh Bibles was acute. The Bibles that were available were mostly in parish churches or in the houses of the gentry.[3]

Another reason for the early success of Methodism in this area was the influence of visiting preachers, especially some of the main revivalist leaders of the eighteenth century—men like Howell Harris, Daniel Rowland, Peter Williams, and William Williams, Pantycelyn.

Howell Harris's visits

It was Lewis Rees and Jenkyn Morgan who were instrumental in bringing Howell Harris to preach in the county. Behind Harris's first visit to Llŷn lies an interesting story.

In 1739, concerned over the spiritual condition and discouragement in the Congregational Church in Pwllheli, one of the members, Walter Williams, went all the way to Llanbryn-mair in mid-Wales to invite Lewis Rees (1710–1800) to preach in his church. Towards the end of that year Rees preached in Pwllheli, and after his sermon a group of believers met with him to share their concerns for the church. Rees shared with them the news of revival which had broken out in south Wales through the ministry of Howell Harris, and their response was immediate. Was it possible for Harris to visit them?

Lewis Rees responded kindly, advising them to contact Jenkyn Morgan, who was running a school in Llanuwchllyn, near Bala. A deputation duly went to see Jenkyn Morgan and persuaded him to move to Pwllheli and start a school there. Morgan's work in Pwllheli was blessed, and soon he was instrumental in bringing Howell Harris to the area.[4] On 7 February 1741 Harris arrived in Glasfryn-fawr, Pwllheli, to a warm welcome. Later, he travelled to Tudweiliog in Llŷn, where crowds heard him preach.[5]

On Harris's second visit to the North, in 1747, he concentrated on the area between Penmachno (near Betws-y-coed) and Waunfawr (near Caernarfon), spending only one day in Llŷn. By 1748, four fellowship meetings (*seiadau*) had been established in the county, at Benllech, Tŷ Engan, Tregarnedd and Llangwnadl. That year Siarl Marc reported to the Association in the South concerning the fellowships in Llŷn and pleaded for visits from Harris.[6] A third trip by Harris, in October 1748, included a visit to Rhandir in Llŷn.

In July 1749 he made a fourth visit to the North, preaching again in Rhandir on 20 July. Two days earlier he had preached in Tregarnedd with 'power and blessing'.[7]

Nanhoron

On his fifth and final visit, Howell Harris received a good welcome in Rhandir. What is interesting is that he was still in the North a month later, and that he went to Nanhoron (in Llŷn), which is close to where Capel y Nant would eventually be built. Here Harris enjoyed the fellowship of Lewis Evan. He preached too for three hours, experiencing great freedom in the Holy Spirit as he opened up the verse,

And I will pour on the house of David and on the inhabitants of Jerusalem the Spirit of grace and supplication; then they will look on Me whom they have pierced; they will mourn for Him as one mourns for his only son, and grieve for Him as one grieves for a firstborn.

(Zechariah 12:10)

Harris also reports that he preached in 'private' and in public for a further five hours. It is certain that he stayed in the attractive Plas Nanhoron (Nanhoron Mansion),[8] the gentry house and estate. Persecution of itinerant preachers like Harris decreased significantly in his last two visits.[9]

Over many years, the Word had been sown in Llŷn by different preachers, despite persecution, and Harris's role in this respect was significant. The Dissenters, however, as we have seen in Pwllheli, welcomed Howell Harris, and he in turn spoke of his debt to them.[10] Many of the Dissenters also joined the Methodists.

The five visits that Harris made to the area between 1741 and 1750 must have contributed directly or indirectly to the establishment of churches there. Robert Jones, Rhos-lan, describes him as

> awakening, diligent and successful in his ministry, and many have been called [savingly] through him . . . He did not follow the usual path of preaching but delivered what the Lord gave him, and that mostly in a convicting manner.[11]

We can assume with some confidence that, at least in the area of Nanhoron in Llŷn, Harris's ministry resulted in conversions and in awakening others to seek the Lord.

Having sketched the earlier history, we can now trace the more immediate background to the 1817 revival in this area. There are several distinct stages in the emergence of Capel y Nant, as the following diagram illustrates.

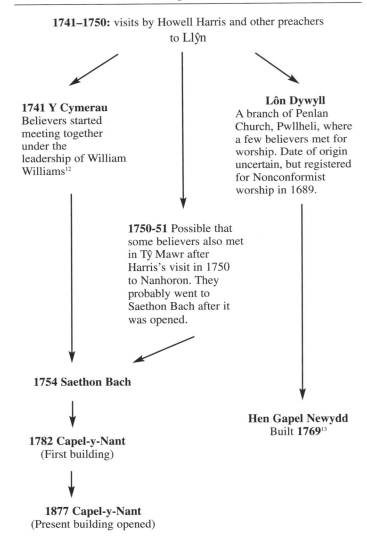

1741–1750: visits by Howell Harris and other preachers to Llŷn

1741 Y Cymerau
Believers started meeting together under the leadership of William Williams[12]

Lôn Dywyll
A branch of Penlan Church, Pwllheli, where a few believers met for worship. Date of origin uncertain, but registered for Nonconformist worship in 1689.

1750-51 Possible that some believers also met in Tŷ Mawr after Harris's visit in 1750 to Nanhoron. They probably went to Saethon Bach after it was opened.

1754 Saethon Bach

1782 Capel-y-Nant
(First building)

1877 Capel-y-Nant
(Present building opened)

Hen Gapel Newydd
Built **1769**[13]

Filling in the details

We can now retrace our steps, filling in some of the details and showing the different stages that led to the eventual emergence of Capel y Nant.

Y Cymerau

It was under the leadership of William Williams that believers started to meet together in Y Cymerau in 1741.[14] Y Cymerau was located about half a mile from Saethon Bach and was literally a smallholding owned by William Williams. Only a few stones remain on the site today, and it is situated in dense woodland so that access is not easy.

The believers met in the home of Williams until the Saethon Bach building was opened in 1754. William Williams was a gifted man, a musician and a godly leader, and he became an elder in Saethon Bach when it was established in 1754. He died in 1770.

Lôn Dywyll

This was a branch of Penlan Welsh Congregational Church in Pwllheli. There is no certainty as to when the cause was established, although it was registered for Nonconformist worship in 1689. Only a small number of believers met here regularly, but Lôn Dywyll had a useful function in providing a Dissenting church with opportunities for Christian fellowship, prayer and the ministry of the Word. This cause gradually became redundant when other church fellowships like Saethon Bach—and especially their own Hen Gapel Newydd—were established.

William Jones, Pandy, claimed that his wife's mother had come from Eifionydd to Lôn Dywyll to worship.[15] Some of the individuals who attended the Lôn Dywyll meetings would have taken a path via Nanhoron Isaf, enjoying a sandwich on the way.

Saethon Bach

David Williams was the son of John Williams, and his parents
had moved to Saethon about 1750. He was a farmer and
landowner with considerable gifts, and also a strong Christian
who delighted in helping people in the locality. He was one of the
leading men who took the decision to build a chapel locally
named Saethon Bach.

This was the first Calvinistic Methodist church to be established in the area. Their aim was not to establish a church, but
rather a preaching station where locals could hear the gospel
preached. Men who were due to preach in the area on the
Sunday—especially, later on, in the Independent Capel Newydd—
would sometimes preach in Saethon Bach on a Saturday evening.
This aim, however, was subsequently modified, and gradually
services began to be held there on a Sunday. But co-operation
was still maintained with Capel Newydd, even when the Saethon
Bach chapel was established and relocated about half a mile
away as Capel y Nant, in 1782.

William Roberts[16] states that the Saethon Bach chapel is no
longer standing. However, within a short distance of the entrance
to Saethon Fawr farm there is a very old thatched bungalow
named Saethon Bach. Could this be the original site and chapel?
The house has been attractively modernised and is rented out in
the summer as a holiday cottage.

Hen Gapel Newydd (translated as 'old New Chapel'!)

This old chapel building is still standing, with windows and
doors intact though in poor condition. It is situated in the
Nanhoron area on the main Pwllheli to Aberdaron road. Driving
to Aberdaron from the direction of Pwllheli, one eventually dis-
covers on the left-hand side a small sign to Capel Newydd. From
this point one needs to walk down a narrow lane for two to three
hundred yards, and then enter a field. The chapel is here on the

left, enclosed and isolated. Alongside it there is an old cemetery, with burials dating back at least as far as 1824.[17] The chapel building itself is small and quaint, but it is dusty and neglected inside. Between the two small doors that give access is a small traditional pulpit, with numerous pews facing it. Approximately a hundred people could have been accommodated inside. The sign near the main road pointing to this chapel records the following details in both Welsh and English:

Addoldy Anghudffurfiol [*sic*]
o'r Ddeunawfed Ganrif
An Eighteenth-Century Dissenters
Meeting House
Capel Newydd
Adeiladwyd 1769   Built 1769

There were close links between this chapel and the longer-established Lôn Dywyll fellowship, which was also a Dissenting Independent cause. Believers in Lôn Dywyll longed for a better building and church where they could develop the work, but they had to wait until 1769[18] before their prayers were answered. It is probable that John Williams, father of the David Williams who helped to establish Saethon Bach, was an elder in Capel Newydd.

Despite belonging to different denominations, there was a degree of co-operation between the Calvinistic Methodist cause at Saethon Bach and the Independent Capel Newydd. For example, in one of the Fellowship meetings in Capel Newydd, probably in early 1782, John Williams proposed to the members that they should give financial assistance to the small church at Saethon Bach in order to enable the believers there to build a new church. That evening, between £40 and £50 was promised by members. This was a generous and unselfish gift for their Calvinistic

45

Methodist brethren, who were building a new chapel reasonably close by.[19]

Initial blessing

There was blessing on the work at Capel Newydd, especially in the earlier years. The exercise of church discipline was not so severe as in the Calvinistic Methodist churches. Some people (the grandmother of William Jones, Pandy, for example) were attracted to Capel Newydd partly because, unlike the Calvinistic Methodists, they baptised all children and did not discipline those who married partners from the world.[20] And there were some well-known local people who joined Capel Newydd.

One such person was Catherine Edwards. She was Lady Nanhoron and lived in the mansion in the area. Her husband, Captain Timothy Edwards, served in thirteen of His Majesty's ships. His last appointment was as Captain of the *Actaeon* in Admiral Rodney's fleet in the West Indies in 1780. On the journey home, and only a week after leaving Barbados, he died from malaria aboard the *Actaeon*. The ship's log records, '. . . by his death his country has lost an honest, gallant officer'.[21]

Unaware of his death, Catherine Edwards went to Portsmouth in 1780 to welcome her husband home, and on receiving the news there she was deeply distressed. In the providence of God, an English Congregational minister in Portsmouth showed her considerable kindness and sought to comfort her through the Bible. The result was that she professed conversion and became a member of the Congregational church in Portsmouth.

On returning to Wales, she joined Penlan Congregational Church in Pwllheli.[22] After Capel Newydd was built, it was appropriate for Catherine Edwards to transfer her membership to the new church, which was close to her mansion home. This influential lady gave considerable support and status to the new Congregational church.

After a few years, however, Capel Newydd as a church was in decline. Following the relocation of the Calvinistic Methodist church from Saethon Bach to Capel y Nant, many adherents and members opted to go there.

Capel y Nant

Capel y Nant was first built in 1782 and was situated less than a mile from Saethon Bach. Remember that believers who had been meeting in Y Cymerau from 1741 had moved to Saethon Bach when it was established in 1754. But the thatch-roofed chapel in Saethon Bach was really only a small house, and this later proved inadequate for the numbers wanting to hear the preaching of the Word, especially when revival broke out there in 1780.

There are no details available as to how this revival started, but two facts are beyond dispute. The first is the spiritual decline among those attending Saethon Bach. This was expressed in indifference to the gospel as well as in some forms of worldliness. It was as though the church had gone to sleep and was 'withering'.[23] Did the elders call for prayer? Or was it the burden of one believer? We do not know the answers to these questions.

The second fact we are sure of is that a powerful local revival broke out here in 1780. Believers were quickened and many unbelievers were converted and added to the church. The need for a new and larger church building became urgent. Eventually in 1782, with financial support from Capel Newydd, Capel y Nant was built just a short distance away. While the number of members was maintained over the following thirty-five years, slowly a general indifference prevailed regarding spiritual matters, and the means of grace in the church at Capel y Nant were rarely effective.

We are now in a position to describe how the Lord came to this church in power and revival.

5
Revival comes to Capel y Nant

A part from the establishing of the Sunday school in the early 1800s, the cause at Capel y Nant made no significant spiritual progress for a number of years. The number of church members was maintained, but both within and outside the church there was a considerable amount of discouragement and indifference. Thankfully, the preaching of the Word in church services was consistently biblical and the Bible was diligently taught in the Sunday school.[1] Sadly, however, people were not being converted and there was no apparent spiritual fruit. Those who listened to the preaching seemed hard and insensitive to the gospel; the young people, too, were rebellious and even wild on occasions.

During the year 1815, a few Christians in the church became concerned about the church's spiritual state and the ineffectiveness of the means of grace. One church elder in particular was deeply disturbed by the situation. His name has not been preserved, though Henry Hughes[2] is reasonably certain it was Hugh Williams the Factory, whose father William Williams had led the fellowship in Cymerau many years previously, before becoming an elder in the Saethon Bach Church. What is certain is that the man was both a church elder and leader of the Sunday school in Capel y Nant. It was in the autumn of 1815 that he urged the Sunday school pupils who were able to read, to study and learn a catechism, with its many questions and answers relating to Bible teaching. The Catechism he commended to the Sunday

48

school was Thomas Charles's *Yr Hyfforddwr* (The Instructor), which had been published only in 1807.

Yr Hyfforddwr

We need to pause at this point to describe this work, so as to see why the Sunday school pupils were being urged to study and learn it. It was one of many catechisms[3] produced in the eighteenth and nineteenth centuries, but in terms of its style and the extent of its influence this was by far the most effective of all the catechisms in nineteenth-century Wales. Both its questions and its answers were more acceptable in terms of their clarity, brevity and directness.

One fact is immediately apparent. Before publishing his catechism in 1807, Thomas Charles had already gained some years of valuable experience in questioning children in day and Sunday schools concerning the Christian faith. His catechism became 'one of the most popular books of the century'[4] in Wales, and before the end of the nineteenth century it had been printed as many as eighty-five times! Even in 1884 William Williams, Swansea, could claim that it 'continues to this day to be extensively used in the Principality'.[5] No wonder Edward Griffiths claimed that, alongside Charles's *Geiriadur* (*Bible Dictionary*), the *Instructor* was 'of such merit as to deserve a place amongst Welsh classics'.[6]

In terms of theology, the *Instructor* was Calvinistic and had been influenced by another Calvinistic catechism,[7] which was the product of the Westminster Assembly of 1642–7. It is no exaggeration to say that, over decades in the nineteenth century, many thousands of Welsh people had been steeped in biblical, Calvinistic teaching by means of such catechisms as the *Instructor*.[8]

This kind of catechism was urgently needed by Thomas Charles at the beginning of the nineteenth century. In addition to the day and night schools that he helped to establish for teaching young and old to read the Bible in Welsh, Sunday schools attached to Calvinistic Methodist and Nonconformist churches also grew rapidly in number and influence in Wales from 1800 onwards. These all-age Sunday schools were extremely useful and popular. Books, then, were urgently required for the benefit of both teachers and pupils. Two such books written by Thomas Charles were the *Instructor* and the *Dictionary*, the latter being affectionately known in Welsh as *Geiriadur Charles*.

Content

The *Instructor* is a valuable and extremely useful book; it contains seventeen chapters with as many as 271 questions and answers, and has a concluding section of five questions relating to the Ten Commandments which people were also expected to learn. The seventeen chapters cover major Bible teaching concerning God, Creation, the Fall, the Person of Christ, the Two Covenants (works and grace), the Offices of Christ as Prophet, Priest and King, Faith and Justification, the Work of the Holy Spirit, the Law of God, the Means of Grace, the Sacraments of Baptism and the Lord's Supper, Christ's Resurrection and Exaltation, the General Resurrection and then the Day of Judgement. By far the longer chapters are those relating to Christ's offices (48 questions), the work of the Holy Spirit (34 questions) and God's law (28 questions).

Many of the answers are memorably brief and direct, but they normally include a Bible verse. For example, to the question 'Who made you?' the answer is simply 'God', but it is followed by Psalm 100, verse 3. Referring to the Holy Trinity of Divine Persons, question 5 is: 'Is each of these persons true God?' 'Yes,' is the response, 'co-equal and co-eternal.' Here is an excellent way of learning Christian doctrine and, at the same time, memorising Bible verses.

However, some of the answers are more detailed. Question 43, for example, relating to Genesis 2:17, is: 'What are we to understand by this death?' Three types of death are then distinguished and described, together with Bible references:

(1) The *Spiritual death* of the soul, that is, his entire departure from God (Ephesians 2:1; John 5:24);

(2) *Natural death*, that is, the separation of soul and body from each other for a season (Hebrews 9:27);

(3) *Eternal death*, that is, all that shall be endured in soul and body for sin to eternity (Romans 6:33; Matthew 25:46; Revelation 21:8).

One of the longest answers is to question 67, relating to the differences between the Covenant of Works and the Covenant of Grace; in this five detailed points are made. Or consider question 148: 'By what names is this change called in Scripture?' Here six answers are provided, using biblical terms and verses to describe regeneration: '*new birth*'; a '*resurrection*'; a '*new creation*'; the '*circumcision of the heart*'; the '*giving of a new heart and a new spirit*', and '*putting the law into the mind, and the writing of it in the heart*'. In each case, of course, the appropriate Bible verse is quoted in full.

Even a superficial reading of the *Instructor* will impress upon readers the broad range as well as the depth of biblical teaching in this catechism. Here is Bible teaching in a catechetical form that can be easily memorised and recalled by pupils, but can also be used by teachers and exhorters in a number of ways, in order to expand and impress the Word upon their pupils' minds and consciences.

A positive response

Now it was a copy of this *Instructor* that the church elder and Sunday school superintendent in Capel y Nant had obtained; and he had no doubt benefited from using it himself. Was this a book that might also help others? His mind was made up, so he asked all those in the Sunday school who were able to read to give themselves personally, and as families, to learning the *Instructor*. The request was heeded, and during the winter of 1815–16 a significant number of people decided to learn the Scripture truths contained in this catechism. For nearly a year the *Instructor* was the main study book used by adults and children in Capel y Nant alongside the Bible. The response was more positive and consistent than the church elder could have expected, but still the church itself was not being aroused spiritually in the way he longed to see.

By the following summer (1816) this elder was still feeling concern for the state of the church. One of his concerns was that all the hard work of preaching, teaching and catechising over the long winter months would prove fruitless, and he was too distressed to allow that to happen.[9] For that reason he took the initiative and called all the church members together. After sharing his concerns, he urged each member to allocate some time each day to prayer, pleading specifically with the Lord to visit the church by the Holy Spirit and prosper the Word. The church elder reinforced his request by warning them that in the next church members' meeting he would ask everyone whether or not they had prayed each day for revival. His conviction was that the saving and reviving power of the Lord is sovereignly expressed through the means of grace, but that it was the responsibility and privilege of the church to seek the Lord in this respect.

Calls to prayer

The wider context of this call to prayer needs to be described at this point. The Rev. Owen Thomas of Liverpool provides a useful summary of the historical background.[10]

Only three years earlier the Association held in Pwllheli[11] had discussed in detail, and with the utmost seriousness, the necessity of praying for the success of the gospel in Wales and in foreign countries. And it was at this time that the tradition was first established among all the Calvinistic churches in Wales that a prayer meeting be held on the first Monday of each month for the preaching of the gospel in other countries as well as Wales.

While the Capel y Nant elder was probably aware of, and constrained by, the Association's emphasis on prayer in 1813, he may also have been aware of emphases on prayer in other situations and countries even earlier. Owen Thomas, for example, refers to what happened in London prior to the outbreak of the great eighteenth-century Methodist revival. In 1712 a number of godly believers and ministers in the city felt such a need for a visitation from the Lord in their churches that they published a paper, *A Serious Call from the City*, for the country to set aside one hour from 7 a.m. to 8 a.m. each Tuesday morning in secret prayer for the Lord's work in Britain and overseas.

Twenty years later in 1732, and again in 1735, a lecture on the same subject was published in Scotland. Many hundreds of Christians agreed to pray privately to the Lord for revival. In 1744, a Union was formed in Scotland, then further afield, to pray for revival and for special manifestations of divine power in saving sinners. Many hundreds of letters were circulated, inviting the Lord's people in different denominations to hold prayer meetings at a convenient time each Saturday evening and Sunday morning, with a special prayer meeting, in addition, on the first Tuesday of each quarter of the year, commencing in October 1744.

Jonathan Edwards

Hearing of this development in Scotland, Jonathan Edwards responded by publishing his *Humble Attempt to Promote Explicit Agreement and Visible Union of God's People in Extraordinary Prayer for the Revival of Religion and the Advancement of*

Christ's Kingdom on Earth.[12] In his *Humble Attempt*, as it is often respectfully described, Jonathan Edwards refers to the willingness of many in Scotland at this time to agree to pray for revival, and to pray initially for a period of two years.[13] The purpose of praying is described by Edwards:

> . . . that he would *appear in his glory*, and favour Zion, and manifest his compassion to the world of mankind, by an abundant effusion of his *Holy Spirit* on all the churches, and the whole habitable earth, to revive true religion in all parts of *Christendom*, and to deliver *all nations* from their great and manifold spiritual calamities and miseries, and bless them with the unspeakable benefits of the kingdom of our glorious Redeemer, and *fill the whole earth with his glory.*[14]

It was just after the end of this initial two-year period of prayer that Edwards wrote his *Humble Attempt*, to promote continuing, earnest supplication for these aims by providing 'motives' and reasons from Scripture, especially unfulfilled prophecies, to encourage believers to pray prevailingly in this way.

After briefly mentioning the London, then Scottish, movements for prayer and Edwards's attempt 'to support this effort',[15] Owen Thomas reports that so great was the faith of believers in that earlier period in the effectiveness of prayer and their own commitment to special prayer for the success of the gospel, that George Whitefield could note in his diary for 28 March 1739: 'I had the pleasure of hearing that over a hundred people had set aside a day [per week] to pray for me and my dear brother, Howel Harris.'[16] No wonder, Thomas exclaims, that such men did such mighty deeds for their God, when over a hundred godly people agreed together to pray each day for them!

Probably all this information was known to the elders at Capel y Nant, and one of them at least had felt constrained to challenge the church members to agree to pray daily in secret for gospel success and revival in their midst.

A spirit of prayer

About a month later, the church members' meeting was convened again and, true to his word, the elder questioned them as to whether they had been praying each day for revival. Encouragingly, he found that all the members except one had done so. Furthermore, they were all agreed that it was of the Lord that they should continue praying corporately, but also privately and daily, for revival in Capel y Nant. They all felt assured that it would not be long before the Lord answered their prayers. A burden for prayer was emerging within this small fellowship. Unexpectedly, however, the burden for prayer was soon to be shared by some of the children and young people—and here we pick up the story with which the book began.

In this early period in the history of the church at Capel y Nant, the Sunday preaching service was normally held at 2 p.m. and the Sunday school started in the late afternoon or early evening. This was a convenient arrangement for obtaining preachers, and also for the local people. Some families living near the church would go home for an hour or two, while others, especially the children, stayed in the church waiting for the Sunday school to commence. One result of this arrangement was that the children and young people tended to be left to themselves, and they became disorderly and noisy in their behaviour.

At the beginning of the winter of 1816 one naughty youngster who was lame had grown tired of the company of his friends and just wanted peace and quiet on his own between the end of the preaching service and the commencement of Sunday school. But what could he do to obtain privacy? To go home was not practicable, as he lived some distance away from the church. He had an ingenious idea. The loft in the small church building seemed an excellent place to resort to, and that is what he did.

The plan worked well for a short while, until, first, a girl, and then others, joined him. One source[17] claims that the other children noticed where he went and tried by various means to join him, but failed. The girl, partly because of her persistence, was the first one permitted to climb up, on condition that she did not trouble him and make a noise.

In the providence of God, it appears that as soon as the girl[18] joined him in the chapel loft, both were constrained to pray. Soon, other children were allowed to join them, and their numbers slowly increased. A spirit of earnest prayer came upon the children and young people, and no one wanted to miss this time together. So enjoyable and important to them were these times of prayer that they decided to meet during the week as well. Their meeting place, on a gorse-covered slope in the vicinity of the church, was to be another secret place of prayer for them. The undisciplined, wild behaviour of the children had given way to prayer and godly fear.

Adults, too, continued in prayer for revival; some were deeply burdened, and some spent nights in prayer. One widow, for example, spent many nights pleading with the Lord for family and neighbours. Her prayers for her prodigal son in Anglesey were answered in a dramatic way.

Signs of change

By January 1817 a spirit of fervent prayer permeated the whole church; corporate and private prayer were given priority and time by the Christians. And now there were signs that prayers were being answered. People had a greater desire to attend the preaching services and they listened attentively. The preaching was accompanied with unusual authority and power. In one service the girl who had joined the lame boy in the chapel loft broke out in weeping, and then in fervent praise of the Lord. A number of others joined her, and the awesome presence of God was felt by the congregation.

Within a couple of weeks there were as many as twenty conversions; then followed others, young and old, for weeks. Unbelievers in the community were also affected; under intense conviction of sin, they were unable to pursue their work, or eat and sleep. Wherever unbelievers were—in bed, at home, in the fields or on the road—the same conviction of sin gripped many of them.

The story is told, for example, of a servant in Nanhoron mansion whose main work it was to clean and care for the horses in the stables. Suddenly, one day, he was overcome by the fear of God, and he trembled and cried pitifully for mercy. Many of the other young male servants were then affected, falling to their knees on the ground and pleading for their lives to be spared by the Lord. There was, of course, opposition, and the stable servant was reported to Colonel Richard Edwards, the owner of the vast estate. But he refused to dismiss him on religious grounds: 'I would rather have him praying than cursing the horses as he has usually done,'[19] was his response.

The felt presence of God permeated the community. Conversions were numerous and life-transforming, occurring among all age groups. The church, too, was ablaze with fervent love and zeal for the Lord. Revival had come at last to Capel y Nant, and it effected enormous changes. But this is only the beginning, as we shall see in the following chapters.

6
Revival approaches Beddgelert

There is an important link between the revival that broke out in Capel y Nant in the Llŷn peninsula early in 1817 and the one that was experienced a little later that same year in Beddgelert. This link needs to be underlined if we are to appreciate the historical progress of the 1817 revival in north-west Wales. To help us to understand the connection between Capel y Nant and Beddgelert, it is necessary to explain how the Calvinistic Methodist churches were governed.

Usually, each local church had elders chosen by its own members. Permission to proceed in the matter of electing elders was first given by the Monthly Meeting (in Welsh, *Cyfarfod Misol*), and often 'two or three persons shall be sent to advise and assist the church in choosing them'.[1] The Monthly Meeting itself was attended by approved preachers and elders of Calvinistic Methodist churches or 'Private Societies' within a clearly defined geographical area. These Monthly Meetings were important and their responsibilities were varied. In addition to holding public services for the preaching of the gospel, they were required to engage in private discussion and sharing as church leaders, to enquire into 'the religious condition' of the place where they met, as well as

speaking to some . . . ministers and . . . elders . . . concerning their experience of saving truths, their spiritual-mindedness, their growth in grace, the consistency of their lives, and their method of leading the flock of Christ. All necessary admonition, encouragement, and instruction, should be given them . . .[2]

The Monthly Meeting was also responsible for the oversight of all the churches and societies in its district, settling disputes, monitoring the preaching and preachers' itineraries, ensuring doctrinal fidelity and assessing the qualifications of candidates for the ministry.

These responsibilities were so extensive that the Monthly Meeting exercised a powerful and positive influence over the affairs of local Calvinistic Methodist churches in their area. And in the providence of God, prior to the major expansion of their churches in north-west Wales, the Capel y Nant and Beddgelert Calvinistic Methodist churches belonged to the same Monthly Meeting.

January, 1817

At the Monthly Meeting held during the second half of January 1817, one of the elders present from Capel y Nant shared in detail the exciting news of revival in his church. Elders present from other churches were encouraged and challenged, including an elder from the church at Beddgelert. Once again we cannot say with certainty who this elder was, but we do know[3] that two more men had been appointed some months previously to serve as elders there.

Richard Roberts, Cae'r Gors, was one of these two men: well educated in the Scripture, he had an exceptional gift in prayer and would have been a considerable help to the church at this time. The other man appointed to the eldership was John Jones, a weaver by occupation, who had moved from Trawsfynydd to Nanmor. He became well-known throughout north and south Wales for his involvement in the Lord's work and his arranging of meetings for itinerant preachers. Through these men, and others, the Lord was blessing the Beddgelert church and preparing it for revival.

Whichever church elder or elders from Beddgelert attended that Monthly Meeting, one of them was so moved by what he heard concerning the Lord's work in Capel y Nant that he resolved to share the news with his own church members. A members' meeting was called, and the entire fellowship was delighted to hear of the revival taking place in Capel y Nant, little more than twenty miles away. The news acted as a stimulus to the believers to seek God in prayer for a similar revival in their church. Despite weaknesses in the church, there was 'one outstanding flower'[4] there, namely, brotherly love linked to a unity of spirit. They felt encouraged to pray privately and corporately, believing that the Lord was able to answer their prayers. And answer their prayers he did! Within a period of three years from 1817 to 1820 there was a 500 per cent increase in their church membership, as people were converted and added to the church during the revival.

Indications of blessing

But when and how were their prayers answered? The first indication of change was almost immediate, within a couple of weeks. It was apparent in the public services, including those on Sundays, when there was a degree of authority and power upon the preaching of the Word. Believers, too, now had greater enjoyment and spiritual profit from the means of grace; they were aware of a gracious quickening in their lives and joy in the Lord. Despite these encouragements, however, there was still no sign that a powerful revival was going to take place.

Another encouraging indication of blessing was in the spring of 1817, when something unusual happened. A man requested membership in the church, and this as a result of the Lord's gracious dealings in bringing him to faith in Christ. This man had not been to the church before and, to the amazement as well as the joy of the congregation, there were clear evidences of the Holy Spirit's saving work in his life.[5]

Only a few weeks later, in early summer, another three adults sought membership. In their case they had attended the church and sat under the preaching of the gospel for years, but only now were they converted. For over twenty-five years the church membership in Beddgelert had remained static at about forty; so to have *four* converts and new members was exceptional and a cause for rejoicing. The number of hearers in the meetings was also increasing, albeit slowly.

Up to this point there is agreement on the part of historians concerning the order of events leading up to revival in Beddgelert. There is also strong evidence[6] that the Hafod y Llan preaching service so signally blessed of God occurred in August 1817. We will describe this important milestone almost immediately.

First, however, we need to pause briefly and inform readers that extant primary sources describing the outbreak of revival in Beddgelert are few in number. Secondary sources, especially material from some later nineteenth-century historians, are unreliable in describing certain aspects of the Beddgelert revival, and it will be necessary in appropriate places to question, and even disprove, some of these details, and even the names of one or two individuals. For this reason we need to move forward cautiously, using the primary and most reliable sources for our data.

Hafod y Llan

As we have seen, from the Monthly Meeting in January 1817 to early summer in the same year, believers in the Beddgelert church had been challenged and constrained to pray daily for the Lord to prosper the means of grace and revive the church. Some answers to their prayers were received in the spring and early summer, but now greater things were to happen in answer to prayer.

It was a Sunday evening in August, possibly the first Sunday in the month, and a preaching service had been arranged to take place in Hafod y Llan, with Richard Williams, Brynengan, as the preacher. This was to be a memorable night: in the words of Henry Hughes, it was 'a great and important night',[7] not just for the area of Beddgelert or for Gwynedd, but also for the whole of Wales. Hughes likens it to 'a storm of lightning and thunders, coming suddenly and very abruptly',[8] and as a result changing the religious and moral climate of Wales.

The location was a small farmhouse at the foot of Snowdon, the highest mountain in Wales and the second largest in the United Kingdom. One historian describes the farmhouse as 'standing in the Gwynant glen, which winds up from Beddgelert, along the base of Snowdon'.[9] No one expected the service to be anything but ordinary, for Richard Williams, though sincere and sound in doctrine, did not have a name as a powerful or popular preacher; he was considered just an average preacher.

One tradition claims that the powerful preacher John Elias was preaching that same evening only about seven miles away in Tremadog, and that some of the locals opted to listen to Elias rather than Richard Williams. But this tradition is clearly wrong. A careful look at John Elias's preaching engagements indicates that he did not preach in Tremadog until 30 October in the Sunday evening service, after preaching earlier that day in Beddgelert.[10] Further, for many years the widow of the Rev. John Jones, Tremadog, kept accurate details[11] of each sermon preached in Tremadog, and it is unlikely that she would have forgotten to record details of a sermon by John Elias.

The testimony of eyewitnesses
One man born and brought up in the area of Beddgelert who witnessed this revival was William Humphrey. He describes for us the scene in Hafod y Llan. The preaching service, he informs us,

was held in the kitchen to the left of the front door. And the room was full. Richard Williams stood between the window and the fire.[12] In the milking room next door a group of uninterested young people were sitting and playing, so he stood on a bench near the table in order to be seen and heard. The opening part of the service was ordinary[13] and the congregation appeared somewhat lifeless and indifferent.

John Jones, Glan Gwynant, was another local person who witnessed the revival.[14] According to Jones, the preacher's text[15] was taken from John 6:44—'No man can come to me, except the Father which hath sent me draw him: and I will raise him up at the last day.'[16]

The Rev. Robert Ellis also attended this meeting; he was then a young boy, nine years of age. According to Ellis, within fifteen minutes of announcing his text the Holy Spirit came upon the preacher. 'It was awful', he writes, and

> impossible to describe. For although Richard Williams was speaking, yet somehow it was not Richard Williams; the voice was not his . . . and the sermon was not his sermon! The preacher had his own sermon on the text and had preached it frequently before. His thoughts in that sermon were instructive, but it was not the old sermon that came out now but a completely new sermon, one he did not possess beforehand and one he could never again afterwards get hold of.[17]

Robert Ellis was in no doubt about it. 'Someone else was speaking to the conscience of the congregation and the old preacher lost himself in him.'[18]

The farmhouse at Hafod y Llan was immediately filled with the sense of God's presence. All the people present, including the young people next door, became serious, earnest, and visibly shaken. John Jones reports that some were weeping because of their sinful condition before God;[19] some cried profusely and uncontrollably. Others rejoiced and wept simultaneously as they praised God for his mercy and salvation extended to them. Hard hearts had been softened[20] and the grace of repentance given to a goodly number there.

At the end of his sermon, Richard Williams prayed before announcing the verse of a hymn for the congregation to sing. But no one sang and the service ended quietly, with some individuals weeping, albeit quietly. William Roberts reports[21] that the people were gripped by such seriousness and fear that they were unable to sing. They eventually went out in silence, frightened by the awareness of God's presence and preoccupied with thoughts concerning the terrors of divine judgement. The young people, too, were similarly affected by the fear of God and became engrossed with spiritual issues that focused on their personal relationship to God.

On the way to their homes, the usual chatter and hilarity were absent and hardly anyone wanted to talk.[22] Even the preacher was amazed at what had happened. In fact, such was the freedom and power with which Richard Williams had been enabled to preach that he felt uncertain whether he *had* preached or whether he was listening to someone else.[23]

The following weeks

For many in the now scattered congregation, that Sunday night was a sleepless night. Monday, too, was a dark day for them, as spiritual concerns took priority over daily work and family duties. For some of them there appeared to be no spiritual comfort or light.[24] But gradually people began to talk to each other about the Sunday evening service; they read the Scriptures and prayed in their homes, and then some individuals began to rejoice because of their new experience of grace and forgiveness. For the converts, their new-found faith pervaded all that they did.

Farm labourers, for example, praised the Lord while milking and working in the fields. Similarly, two young men travelling from Nant Gwynant to the village of Beddgelert in a horse-drawn cart began to talk freely together about the Lord Jesus Christ. Within minutes, they were so deeply moved by thoughts of the glory of Christ's person and his unique sacrifice for sinners on the cross that they began spontaneously to shout praises to the Lord.[25]

On the Sunday evening following the remarkable preaching service in Hafod y Llan, a prayer meeting was due to be held in the same farmhouse. Two miles away, a couple of teenage girls were wondering what they could do that would be different that evening, wanting to enjoy themselves and have a laugh. They hit on the idea of going to the prayer meeting to laugh at those believers who would be shouting praises to the Lord. They went, but on the way home they themselves were crying and calling out loudly for mercy until midnight, and one of them at least was soundly converted.[26]

Within a period of five weeks, almost every home in the Nant Gwynant area of the large Beddgelert parish had been affected to some degree by this revival. But as there was no church in Nant Gwynant itself, scores of these converts and those who were seeking salvation joined the Calvinistic Methodist church in Beddgelert.

What needs to be appreciated here is that the revival was reaching the village of Beddgelert. Indeed, a unique aspect of this revival was that it did not break out beyond the Nant Gwynant locality 'until it placed its mark on almost all the inhabitants' there.[27] In the next chapter we will trace the way in which the revival reached the village of Beddgelert.

7
Revival reaches Beddgelert

One early tradition in the eighteenth and early nineteenth centuries was for a *seiat* to be held in each Calvinistic Methodist church, fellowship or 'society'. Earlier church leaders had refused to hold a *seiat* immediately after a preaching service, no matter how effective the preaching had been. Their refusal was based on the conviction that the radical work of regeneration and the effectual call was a divine activity entirely, so it was inappropriate to interfere with what God was doing in a person's life. For the Beddgelert church, the *seiat* was held on a weekday. Many of the Methodists' preaching and *seiat* meetings were on weekdays as, until 1811, they had been officially members of the Church of England.

It is not easy to translate the Welsh word *seiat*, but a fellowship or sharing or 'experience' meeting approximates somewhat to its meaning. The aim of such a meeting 'was primarily to provide a fellowship in which the new spiritual life and experience of the people could be safeguarded and developed'.[1] In these fellowship meetings, Dr D. Martyn Lloyd-Jones insists,

> The great emphasis was primarily on experience, and the experimental knowledge of God and His love and His ways. Each member gave an account of God's dealings with him or her, and reported on any remarkable experience, and also their sins and lapses, and so doing compared notes with one another in these respects.

While considerable stress was placed on prayer and reading the Bible, these meetings were not discussion or even Bible-study groups. 'Here, the emphasis was on daily life and living, the fight against the world, the flesh and the devil, and the problems that arise inevitably in the Christian's pilgrimage through this world of sin.'[2]

As we saw in the previous chapter, for four or five weeks following the remarkable Hafod y Llan meeting in early August, where Richard Williams preached such a powerful sermon, the revival was confined to the Nant Gwynant area of the parish. One *seiat* or 'sharing' meeting[3] following the Hafod y Llan service was unusually blessed. Although the Calvinistic Methodists had three preaching centres in this scattered parish, the only chapel building was in the village of Beddgelert. It was here in the chapel that the sharing meeting was held, early in the week and at midday. Two of the church elders were present: Rhys Williams, Hafod y Llan, and William Williams, Hafod y Rhisgl.

A remarkable *seiat*

The two elders were waiting in the adjoining chapel house for the meeting to start. One of them opened the door into the chapel to see if the faithful few believers who regularly attended had arrived. A shock awaited him. Instead of the normal handful of people, the chapel was crowded. He turned back and reported to his colleague, 'It is certain that the people have misunderstood; they are expecting a sermon; the chapel is full and all the people of the parish are here.'[4]

This, of course, was an exaggeration. The chapel was full, but it would never have accommodated the 747 persons registered as living in the parish according to the 1811 census.[5] What the elder was expressing (and Henry Hughes is correct in suggesting this)[6] was his shock in seeing so many people, including all kinds of people he would never expect to see at such a meeting.

The two elders proceeded immediately into the chapel and the meeting commenced with a Bible reading. Then, as the verse of a hymn was being sung, many in the congregation were overwhelmed. Some cried for mercy; others rejoiced in their salvation in Christ; some prayed or sang praise; but, adds Robert Ellis, 'No one thought of order.'[7] Eventually the people were persuaded to go to their homes, and news of the event spread throughout the neighbourhood.

The Sunday school

It was later in September 1817 that the revival flooded the village of Beddgelert. The occasion was the fair which was due to be held in the locality on 21 September.[8] On the Sunday before the fair,[9] God visited the church in power, and once again it was unexpected and awesome. The scene for this divine visitation was the all-aged Sunday school. One class of young women was deeply affected, especially when reading the last chapter of John's Gospel. Unusually, the young women were gripped by the verses in the chapter and quietly wept, unable to continue the Bible reading.

Some minutes later, the different classes reassembled and it was the turn of Richard Roberts, Cae'r Gors, to address and question the whole Sunday school before it ended. Richard Roberts, a church elder and Sunday school superintendent, was a godly Christian with a gracious attitude. He was full of zeal for the success of the gospel and had a deep concern both for the spiritual growth of believers and the conversion of unbelievers. That afternoon, however, he felt a special burden for the young people. And the reason? The fair was due in the area for one day that week, and he knew only too well how it would encourage worldliness, drunkenness and immorality.

Possibly, Richard Roberts had heard Christian leaders like the Rev. Thomas Charles speak against these fairs, advising parents and church leaders to discourage young people from attending them. Only six years earlier in 1811, for example, Thomas Charles had given a major address to Sunday school teachers and scholars, warning of the danger of fairs.

Thomas Charles's address

Charles's main concern was to show that 'the ordinances of the Lord Jesus have been appointed for the promotion of his great cause in the salvation of sinners,' namely, *'the preaching of his Word—baptism—the Lord's Supper—and prayer'*. Charles continued, 'By these means, chiefly, he calls, feeds and comforts his people . . .', but it is 'religious madness to expect a blessing in any other way than that which he has appointed.'[10]

After explaining the nature, purpose and right use of these ordinances, Thomas Charles used the opportunity to emphasise that the *'Devil has his ordinances* as well as Christ, in this world', by which he 'maintains and advances the interest of his corrupt and ruinous kingdom'.[11] And what are these ordinances that the devil uses? Charles is in no doubt about the answer. Such ordinances are 'all the corrupting customs and practices of our country, such as card-playing, dancing, wakes, feasts, revelling, drunkenness, etc. . . . and [they] continue to one or two o'clock in the morning'. Thomas Charles then urges the Sunday school teachers to 'warn the children most seriously on the subject'.

But there was 'one thing particular on my mind to mention here,' adds Charles; 'that is, the common practice of letting children and young people go to fairs and markets . . . to idle and to follow vanity'.[12] He speaks at this point from experience in monitoring and developing the day and sabbath schools. 'One fair', he claims, 'often disorders a school for a quarter of a year. After bringing guilt and shame on themselves at the fair, they cannot for a long time after join in carrying on the work of the Lord.' For parents to take their children to a fair is 'a foolish practice', remarks Charles; 'rather let them show them the danger, vanity and sinfulness of such useless and corrupting habits and customs'. And for the Sunday school teachers, Thomas Charles desires that they show the children 'how vile, unseemly, dangerous and sinful are the ordinances of the Devil'. On the other hand, they must also show them 'how beautiful, desirable and blessed are the ordinances of God'.[13]

There was also some good news for Charles to report: 'The ordinances of Satan are entirely abolished in some parts of the country, and that going to fairs and such things are wholly given up. What has been done in some places', he declares, 'may by the Lord's blessing be done in other parts.'[14]

A solemn warning

Richard Roberts was probably familiar with the details of this and other addresses by Thomas Charles concerning the spiritual and moral dangers posed by such fairs. And now a fair was due to be held in their parish. Burdened for the young people, he dutifully warned them not to go to the fair that week.

He repeated the warning again and again. His words assumed considerable authority, and the entire Sunday school listened intently. Then he quoted some words from an old Welsh hymn.[15] The Welsh words are, '*Mae'r afael sicraf fry*'. It is not easy to capture the force of this in English, but it can be literally translated as 'The surest hold's on high.'

What the Sunday school superintendent did was to underline and use repeatedly the small Welsh word '*fry*', which appears at the end of the Welsh version of the hymn and can be translated 'on high'. The English translation of what Roberts said as he stressed this word is as follows: 'Everything of value comes to us from *on high*' (italics mine). 'From *on high*', he continued, 'come light, heat and rain.' And 'from *on high* come blessings of salvation to the earth'. Again and again he emphasised the point:

'From *the heights* God pours his Holy Spirit . . . here is hope for the hard men of Beddgelert . . . If it is dark here,' he stressed, 'it is light *on high*; if it is weak here, it is firm and solid *on high*.'[16]

With these words, the Holy Spirit fell on everyone in the Sunday school, old and young, believer and unbeliever. The weeping filled the whole building; it was intense but quiet and subdued; very few broke out in rejoicing on this occasion. All the people felt the presence of God in the building in a frightening way. One boy ran home to his father, shouting, 'Father, the day of judgement has come!'

The village of Beddgelert was now in revival, but it would not be contained there. The revival was about to spread throughout the entire parish, and further afield to many villages and towns in north Wales.

8
Revival power and heavenly singing

Following the exceptional Sunday school meeting in the Beddgelert chapel, the revival spread rapidly and powerfully through the village and Nant Colwyn up to Drws-y-coed, where the Moravians had once met for a brief period.[1] The immediate result was that the small Calvinistic Methodist church became crowded; almost everyone wanted to attend the meetings. One practical solution involved the arranging of at least two, and sometimes three, meetings during the week, in order to deal with all those individuals expressing concern over spiritual matters, such as awareness of personal sin and perceived need for a right relationship with God through Jesus Christ. Another purpose of the additional meetings was to prepare some of these people for church membership.

In Beddgelert, as in other areas of the parish, the lives of many individuals and families were gloriously transformed by the grace of God. Men of all ages and backgrounds were converted, as well as women, young people and children. 'In the middle of the dark night of discouragement' for the area of Beddgelert, reports Robert Jones, Rhos-lan, 'the people have seen a great light.'[2] As one who had witnessed a number of other revivals in his lifetime, the testimony of this man about the Beddgelert revival is significant:

No one remembers seeing such conviction and unction so powerfully accompanying the means of grace as in this area and many other areas. The convictions were so strong in awakening and pricking the conscience and the showers of rejoicing in salvation so powerful that they have never been seen in revivals before.[3]

While allowing for an element of exaggeration in this statement, the underlying point is nevertheless sound, namely, that the Beddgelert revival appeared to many contemporaries, even to some historians, as at least comparable to any other revival known in Wales. For some, the power evident in dealing mercifully with local people appeared to be unique in terms of its intensity and impact. In fact, such was the effect of the Word of God on the lives of people in Beddgelert that Robert Ellis suggested it would have been worth the angels in heaven organising a trip to Beddgelert in order to see what a glorious work the grace of God was accomplishing in the lives of lost, guilty sinners![4]

But many visitors did come, from near and far, to witness first-hand what was happening in this revival. Usually, those who visited the village were also affected. In later chapters we will see how young men like Cadwaladr Owen from Dolwyddelan were dealt with by God when attending a preaching meeting in Beddgelert.

'The Lord was obviously with his people'

Such was the power and presence of God felt in preaching meetings that it was unusual for a preacher to have quiet to finish his sermon, because of the cries and pains of people under conviction of sin, or the unrestricted rejoicing of those who had just tasted the wonder and comfort of forgiveness and peace with God. Robert Ellis remarks that if the preacher had peace to start and continue the sermon, then it would be impossible to finish it unless the preacher himself was spiritually cold.[5] Indeed, whether it was a sharing meeting or a preaching service, a prayer or a hymn or part of a sermon would rekindle the flame of revival, and the congregation would again be overcome by the power of Scripture truths and aspects of the gospel message.

In all the meetings the people were eager to hear the Bible explained and proclaimed. There was such an anointing on all the means of grace that it was easy to preach, easy to pray, and easy to sing the praises of God. This was revival: 'The Lord was obviously with his people; many were converted and Zion was being built up. And the rocks of Snowdonia reverberated with the sounds of song and praise.'[6]

Nanmor

One of the last areas in the parish to be affected by this revival was Nanmor, a distance of only three miles from the village. The precise date on which the revival spread to Nanmor is uncertain. While Henry Hughes says that Nanmor's experience of revival was about three months after the Hafod y Llan meeting in early August, another source dates it a few weeks later, just before Christmas 1817.[7]

In the context of the next incident I shall relate, John Jones, Nanmor, provides us with four interesting details. First, it was in Beddgelert itself that the Calvinistic Methodists established their first church in this large parish. Secondly, the names of church members from the Nanmor area of the parish were included in the one Beddgelert church book. Thirdly, the members from Nanmor and other areas went to Beddgelert regularly each week to the fellowship or *seiat* meeting, as well as to the Sunday evening preaching service. Although this involved walking six to eight miles, they counted it a privilege to do so in view of the blessings they enjoyed under the preaching of the Word and their opportunity on the way home to share together the glorious truths they had heard. And the fourth detail Jones provides concerns the preaching arrangements on the Sunday. The first service was held at 10 a.m. in Tylyrni; the preacher then went to Nant Gwynant for 2 p.m., and to the Beddgelert church in the evening.

As already mentioned, relying on the evidence of John Jones, who lived in Nanmor at the time and witnessed the revival, Henry Hughes tells of a group of young people who decided to go to Tremadog to hear John Elias preach,[8] instead of listening to Robert Sion Hugh in the local venue in Tylyrni. Overhearing them discussing their plans, a godly elderly woman said to them, 'I would not go, for Robert Sion Hugh is as much a true servant of the Lord as is John Elias.'[9]

The young people ignored her advice at first and set off the next day for Tremadog as planned. On the way, however, her words struck them so forcefully that they decided to return and listen to Robert Sion Hugh. When the old lady saw these young people coming in to the local service she was deeply affected, and this in turn had an effect on the preacher. The result was a powerful preaching service, and one that was remarkable for its impact on the congregation.[10]

Tylyrni

Christmas Sunday, 25 December, was a memorable one in Nanmor. Edward Jones, the preacher in the service in Tylyrni, was tired after travelling from Penrhyndeudraeth and, in order to help him, David Jones, Beddgelert, was asked to commence the meeting. He read a passage from the Bible, announced a hymn and then prayed. But it was difficult to lead the meeting and engage in prayer, for the atmosphere was unusually hard and dark. However, while David Jones was still leading the service, a number of people came towards the house called Tylyrni where the service was proceeding. These people were singing. Almost immediately the atmosphere in the service improved and the old preacher, Edward Jones, felt stirred and blessed as he rose to preach. He was given outstanding liberty and power to preach the Word.[11]

Here is one example of the blessing on this service. A young farm labourer had encouraged some of his friends to stand outside the house, making fun of the preacher and the congregation. A group of these young men stood by the door ready to ridicule. But as they listened to Edward Jones preaching with such anointing, the farm labourer who was leader of the group moved slowly nearer to the preacher. The young man was pale and 'trembling with fear and horror, as though summoned to a court of law'.[12] He wept and groaned under conviction of sin. The other young men were similarly affected, while at the same time some of the elderly ladies broke out into loud rejoicing.

'Singing in the air'

And it was here in the Nanmor area of Beddgelert that one of the earliest occurrences of 'singing in the air' or 'heavenly singing' was reported. On Christmas Eve 1817, one man living in Tylyrni tells of his parents going to a church service and leaving his sister and himself to look after the house. At about 9 p.m. he suddenly heard singing immediately above him. He described it as the 'singing of a myriad voices'. Unable to distinguish or understand the words, he said that 'it was sweeter music than he had ever heard before'.[13] He felt almost mesmerised by it and thought his whole body was disintegrating. Unaware of how long the singing had continued, he and his sister went to the door; but the sound was moving in another direction and was soon out of their hearing. As soon as their parents returned home and were told of the heavenly singing, one of them shouted, 'The revival is coming to Nanmor.'[14]

They did not have long to wait. The next day Edward Jones was given exceptional power in preaching the Word. And a week later, on Sunday morning 1 January 1818, William Roberts of Clynnog enjoyed exceptional freedom, as did Richard Williams, Brynengan, on the following Sunday afternoon.

The 'heavenly singing'[15] was a feature of this revival to which many people testified on different occasions. The Tylyrni incident in Nanmor which has just been described was by no means an isolated occurrence.

What was this singing like? John Hughes helps us at this point. He describes it as

> the sound of a thousand and myriad, myriad sweet voices singing—not a particular tune but—a harmony of the most excellent kind, the like of which people have never heard before. The singing left men rooted to the ground on which they stood, overwhelming them completely.[16]

For the benefit of cynics, Hughes adds that those who heard this heavenly singing were most trustworthy and responsible individuals in the churches. Sometimes they would be aware of this singing in the air when standing in a group together outside a church building, or walking home together from a meeting. They would listen for a considerable period of time, until gradually it became more faint, and then faded away completely.

As the revival spread throughout north-west Wales, the heavenly singing was heard in other localities as well. For example, in 1818 a lot of people heard such singing outside a slate quarry near Bangor and described it in this way:

> At the beginning it was heard as if it wafted on the wind far away from us so that it could be scarcely heard. It was a weak sound, melodious with different voices and gradually drawing nearer to several of us until it was heard powerfully, clearly and effectively. Now it was like the sound of a great crowd rejoicing or praising.[17]

The Rev. Evan Richardson, Caernarfon, also refers to two occurrences of heavenly singing during the year 1818. One was after a fellowship meeting on a Saturday evening in Llanberis, when some of the Christians present informed him that they had heard singing in the air. As they described the incident to him, an elder interrupted them and declared, 'There is no such thing at all. Do not be silly.'[18] Before reaching home that evening, however, this same elder heard the heavenly singing and it had a remarkable effect on him.

The second incident was very different. Evan Richardson was walking home from a church meeting when he heard singing in the air. He asked his companions to slow down, and then to stop and listen to the heavenly choirs. One of the men was cynical and denied that there was such a phenomenon. Within minutes, the singing became clearer and more powerful, so that all the men were able to hear it. Richardson, the respected minister, turned to the cynic and asked, 'Thomas, did you hear it?' There was no reply from the man. The question was posed a second time, and again there was no response. Then Richardson noticed that this man, like the others, was completely overwhelmed and subdued; it was impossible for him to speak even a single word.

Some minutes later, after a great effort, Thomas eventually said, 'I hear, thousands and thousands' of voices. 'Why did you not answer me before?' asked Evan Richardson. The reply was predictable: 'O, I could not have spoken even if you had given me the whole world!'[19]

Its effect

In all the different reports and descriptions of this 'singing in the air', no one claimed to have been able to distinguish the words being sung, nor did anyone see any kind of apparition. All they claimed was that it was the sweetest and most glorious singing they had ever heard. While this singing was to them like a large congregation praising God with heavenly music and zeal, yet they emphasised that it was different from everything they had ever heard before.[20] And the effect of hearing such singing was profound and overwhelming, and contributed powerfully to an even deeper reverential awe of God.

Praise and preaching

Not all the Christians in the revival were privileged to hear this singing in the air; it was occasional, and sovereignly confined to specific locations and groups of people.[21] What all the people did hear, however, was the sound of Christians in their homes, villages and churches, and in the open fields, rejoicing and praising the Lord. During the peak of the revival, such praises could be heard in all directions, both day and night. Heaven became more real to people than earth, and the wonders of God's saving grace in Christ evoked intense and prolonged praise and rejoicing from converts. Such spontaneous praise would break out even at midday, as workers gathered hay in the fields or milked the cows.

Essentially, however, it was not singing that was prominent, but preaching. The Beddgelert revival was a *preaching* revival, and in the next chapter we will begin to describe the way in which preachers were used in extraordinary ways to declare the gospel of Christ.

9
Preaching:
its importance

For the Calvinistic Methodists in Wales, preaching was extremely important. One major reason for this was their high view of the Bible. For example, they affirmed that it is 'abundantly evident that the Scriptures come from God, and from no other source'.[1] Having God as their origin and author, the Scriptures are 'a full, sufficient and perfect revelation of the mind and will of God, concerning all things that are necessary to be known for our salvation . . .'[2]

The Calvinistic Methodists rightly claimed that the major Bible message concerns 'salvation', which God himself planned, accomplished, then applies to individuals. From eternity, God sovereignly elected 'in Christ a great multitude . . . out of every . . . nation, to holiness and eternal life'.[3] In the eternal covenant of grace made by 'the blessed Persons of the Trinity—the Father, the Son and the Holy Ghost',[4] the Son, as 'covenant Head and mighty Surety, represents and stands in the stead of all those . . . who are elected and believe in him unto salvation'.[5] Jesus Christ, as the God-man, 'thus redeemed a countless multitude, by making a full atonement for all their sins'.[6]

Proclamation
Preaching was viewed by the Calvinistic Methodists, therefore, as the proclamation of God's Word, and especially of the gospel. John Elias, in an essay entitled 'On preaching the Gospel', explains that preaching the gospel

is to declare and publish *good tidings* respecting the way of saving sinners from their sins and the wrath of God, showing that salvation springs out of the sovereign grace and love of God . . . It is to preach *Christ*, in his person, offices, life, death, resurrection, ascension and intercession. It is to 'preach Christ crucified' . . . to preach the blessings that are to be received through Christ's merits, reconciliation, forgiveness, justification, sanctification, full salvation. It is to publish Christ as everything which a sinner needs . . .[7]

For the Calvinistic Methodists, preaching was the declaration of all that God had spoken in the Bible and done in Christ.

Applying salvation

But they had more to say about the importance of preaching. 'To save sinners,' they insisted, 'it is as necessary to apply as it was to provide the plan of salvation.'[8] Why? Because people in their sin and enmity 'will not accept or make use of it',[9] so that God's salvation 'would have been a vain thing'. No preacher or even angel has the ability to apply salvation; it 'must be applied, as well as provided, by an infinite Person'.[10] The One entrusted to apply salvation is God the Holy Spirit, who 'convinces and regenerates sinners, guides and comforts the children of God, and will raise them up at the last day'.[11] His work in such individuals is supernatural, irresistible, inward and transforming. Or, in the words of the Confession, the Holy Spirit's work in the elect is 'a gracious, holy, effectual and abiding work . . .'[12]

A major principle

Now preaching is crucial in God's method of bringing the elect to Christ and then nourishing and sanctifying them. Not only did God decree all things from eternity and elect many people to be saved, but he also 'appointed all the means necessary to accomplish this end'.[13] One of the 'means' chosen by God is preaching.

Here is a major principle that needs to be understood. Explaining the point further, the 1823 Confession of Faith affirms:

> Christ, the head of the church, has instituted ordinances, means of grace, and an order of worship, to be used in the church by all his people . . . Through these ordinances, God gives grace, and nourishes and increases the grace given. They are the ordinances of *preaching* [italics mine], reading and hearing the word, prayer, praise, mutual instruction, conversation, the exercise of every part of church discipline and the sacraments of Baptism and the Lord's Supper.[14]

Divine election, therefore, does not entail fatalism or a lazy leave-it-to-God attitude on the part of Christians. The very opposite is true, for God has chosen to use specific means such as preaching in order to achieve his purposes.

How, for example, are people regenerated? Once again the answer provided in the Confession is a biblical one: 'It is generally wrought by means of the word.'[15] How are sinners 'called' effectively to Christ? It is 'the power of God [which] works through'[16] the proclamation of the gospel, bringing individuals to trust Christ and enjoy spiritual, intimate union with him. But it is the Word which the Holy Spirit uses. And notice that one mark of the true visible church is that 'the true doctrine is *preached*'[17] (italics mine).

From this brief discussion, we can see that the reasons advocated by Calvinistic Methodists for attaching such importance to preaching are substantial and persuasive. Proclamation of the Word was deemed essential in order to make known to people what God had revealed of himself and his purposes in the Bible. Preaching was also understood by them to be the normal means used by the Holy Spirit to bring the elect to Christ, and then to nourish and sanctify them. Professor Tudur Jones is correct in affirming that, for Calvinistic Methodists as well as for Calvinistic

Baptists and Congregationalists in nineteenth-century Wales, preaching was 'given a crucial role in mediating God's Word and God's actions to sinners'.[18]

In the Pwllheli Association of the Calvinistic Methodists in September 1825, for example, John Elias in his memorial sermon dealt with the subject of preaching and its significance. Among many useful points he made, three are relevant to our discussion. First, he emphasised that purity of doctrine and holiness of life are indispensable for the preacher. Secondly, what was of primary importance was not eloquence or knowledge, but rather 'the gracious presence of the Lord with them'.[19] Thirdly, 'all necessary gifts for the work of the ministry, and for the edification of the body of Christ, lie in the Head of the Church, seated on God's right hand'.[20]

For Elias and many of his Christian contemporaries, therefore, acknowledging Christ's headship was not a mere formality. It was a dynamic and humbling truth, which encouraged them to safeguard standards for preachers and, at the same time, to pray for the Holy Spirit to empower the preaching. Only the Head of the church could do the latter.

Distinguishable periods

A Calvinistic Methodist historian like Edward Griffiths[21] has identified four distinguishable periods in the history of the Welsh denomination during the eighteenth and nineteenth centuries. Griffiths distinguishes first of all the 'Revival Period', 1735–1785, when Howell Harris, Daniel Rowland, William Williams (Pantycelyn), Howell Davies (Pembrokeshire) and David Jones (Llan-gan) were greatly used by the Lord.

This was followed by what Griffiths called the 'Organizing Period', 1785–1811, when men like David Charles, Thomas Charles (Bala) and Thomas Jones (Denbigh) were significant leaders. In this period occurred the development of the Welsh

Sunday school movement, the first ordination of Calvinistic Methodist ministers (1811), Bible distribution and the publication of Christian magazines like the *Spiritual Treasury* (*Trysorfa Ysbrydol*) and books like Charles's *Christian Instructor* (*Yr Hyfforddwr*) and *Dictionary* (*Geiriadur*).

A third period identified by Griffiths is the 'Preaching Period', 1811–1850. In the initial 'Revival Period', writes Griffiths, the leaders 'were great and powerful preachers. Their preaching took the form of a mighty awakening. In them we see the watchman upon the tower sounding the trumpet of warning to the people of the land.'[22] How then did the 'Preaching Period' differ from this 'Revival Period'?

'An army of men'

In the explanation provided by Griffiths I can identify two main differences. One is that the 'Preaching Period gave to the nation a class of preachers . . . an army of men' in abundance. In fact, their number was so 'great'[23] that Griffiths felt that 'to make a selection out of such a number of worthies is a difficult task, and . . . a severe ordeal'.

A second difference between the revival and the preaching periods, according to Griffiths, is that the latter 'was a season when preachers and preaching held sway over the land'.[24] Preachers whom he singles out for mention are: Ebenezer Morris, Tŵr-gwyn (1769–1825); John Elias, Llangefni (1774–1841); Henry Rees, Liverpool (1798–1869); John Jones, Tal-sarn (1796–1857), and Edward Matthews, Ewenny (1813–1892).

The fourth period which Griffiths distinguishes in nineteenth-century Welsh Calvinistic Methodism is the 'Educational Period',[25] from 1850 onwards. In this period, provision was made to meet the perceived need for 'an educated ministry'.[26]

These four periods identified by Edward Griffiths are useful in drawing attention to some of the prominent features and stages in the development of the Calvinistic Methodist denomination in Wales. Nevertheless, one must treat this classification with caution. An obvious reason for caution is that these four periods overlap considerably in terms of emphasis and practice. For example, revivals broke out frequently at local, regional and even national levels outside the first 'revival period' identified by Griffiths (1735–1785), while there was also a considerable amount of organisation occurring in the first as well as in the second and later periods. Furthermore, preaching was a dominant feature in all four periods.

For the purposes of this book, however, Griffiths's fourfold description of Welsh Calvinistic Methodism is helpful. It draws attention to the fact that the Beddgelert revival of 1817–1822 occurred in a period when preaching was in the ascendancy and when it was used remarkably for the growth and nurture of the Lord's work in Wales.

Another factor

There is another aspect, however, one that relates both to preaching and to the Beddgelert revival. In the early part of the nineteenth century, Calvinistic Methodism in Wales was facing a crisis, in that it was losing its major leaders through death. Daniel Rowland, Llangeitho, had died in 1790 and William Williams, Pantycelyn, in 1791. There was a great shortage of ordained ministers and, in consequence of this, 1811 saw the ordination, for the first time, of Calvinistic Methodist ministers outside the Anglican church.

In 1814, just prior to the Beddgelert revival, Thomas Charles of Bala died and, in 1820, Thomas Jones of Denbigh, a renowned theologian. Two other leaders died soon afterwards: Evan Richardson, Caernarfon, in 1824 and Ebenezer Morris, Tŵr-gwyn, in 1825. Losing such outstanding leaders and preachers, the denomination felt itself to be vulnerable.

Once again, the Head of the church provided for his church by giving it a good number of younger preachers. Consequently, during or at the time of the Beddgelert revival, men were raised up as gifted, powerful preachers—men like Henry Rees, John Jones, David Jones, Cadwaladr Owen, Moses Jones, Robert Hughes (Gaerwen) and Robert Owen (Rhyl). The ministries of these men were a great blessing to Wales over the following forty years or more. Edward Parry remarks, 'If the Beddgelert revival had only brought Cadwaladr Owen and John Jones to the Lord, it would have been worthwhile.'[27]

While the Beddgelert revival contributed significantly to the provision of a new and young generation of preachers, the revival itself was also a preaching revival. The Lord used the preaching of his Word powerfully on many occasions during this period to bless his church. It was upon the preaching of Richard Williams, Brynengan, that the revival had broken out in such power in Hafod y Llan. In the next chapters we will describe some of the more memorable and powerful preaching occasions during this revival.

10
Powerful preaching

Powerful, anointed preaching during periods of local, regional and national revivals had been a regular feature in many parts of Wales between 1735 and 1817. And such preaching had been known in north-west Wales prior to the Beddgelert revival.

Robert Roberts, Clynnog

One outstanding example of it was in the ministry of Robert Roberts, Clynnog (1762–1802). His nephew, Michael Roberts, Pwllheli, reported that those who had heard both Daniel Rowland and Robert Roberts were of the opinion that Roberts came closest of all preachers to Daniel Rowland in terms of the power and effectiveness of his preaching. A contemporary of Roberts, who also preached in the area of Beddgelert during the revival of 1817–1822 and was himself an outstanding preacher, was Ebenezer Morris. His testimony concerning Roberts is a remarkable one, for he had also heard Daniel Rowland preach on numerous occasions. 'If I had died without hearing Robert Roberts, Clynnog, preaching,' remarked Morris, 'I would have died without having the idea I have of the glorious ministry of the Gospel.'[1] Owen Thomas, writing of Daniel Rowland in his famous *Cofiant John Jones*, *Tal-sarn,* claimed that 'no one, except Robert Roberts, was more consistently under the obvious signs of heavenly unction'.[2]

Only forty years old when he died, Roberts was converted when sixteen years of age through the powerful preaching of the Anglican clergyman, Rev. David Jones, Llan-gan. On account of a serious illness which affected his spine in his youth, Roberts developed a deformity resulting in his being a hunchback.

In his earlier years he had been employed as a labourer in the slate quarry, before becoming a farm labourer. As he approached his twenty-fourth birthday, a powerful revival broke out in the Brynengan fellowship in Caernarvonshire which he faithfully attended. Roberts himself was greatly blessed and his heart was filled with overflowing love for Christ and for the conversion of unbelievers.

The ministry of the Word in Brynengan was so powerful that in each preaching service, over many months, people were converted and believers themselves were quickened. The sense of God's presence in the church and in the village was overwhelming; night and day believers praised the Lord, both inside and outside their meeting place. Preachers were often surprised at the power that the Word had on the congregation, and in almost every service a spirit of rejoicing broke out.

At the age of twenty-five, Roberts was encouraged to begin preaching. His gifts of oratory and a strong voice, together with his deep spirituality and prayerfulness, contributed to his becoming a commanding preacher. Beyond all question, he frequently preached with great power and pathos. In the county of Caernarvonshire many hundreds were converted through his preaching, and outside Caernarvonshire, whether in Wales or in England, his preaching was accompanied by similar power.

Dr George Lewis

While a great measure of spiritual blessing and reviving was known amongst Calvinistic Methodists at this time, there were also some preachers in Nonconformist denominations who were empowered by the Lord in their preaching. Among the Congregationalists, one unexpected example was Dr George Lewis, the pastor in Llanuwchllyn, near Bala. He was far from being a popular preacher; in fact, his preaching was normally dry and heavy; one of his characteristics was that his hand was always in his waistcoat pocket. But it was under the ministry of Dr Lewis that a most powerful revival broke out in 1806 and 1809. When the Holy Spirit came upon this preacher in the public services, the effects on the congregation were exceptionally powerful. In fact, Henry Hughes doubted whether anything more powerful occurred elsewhere in Wales at this time.[3]

Christmas Evans

Amongst the Baptists, Christmas Evans (1766–1838) was being greatly used in north-west Wales. It was in July 1789 that Evans first moved to Anglesey as a Baptist pastor. From 1776 until his arrival in 1789, about three hundred people had professed conversion and joined Baptist churches in Gwynedd, half of this number being located in Anglesey.[4] Quite soon after the commencement of Evans's ministry in Anglesey, there was a powerful anointing of the Holy Spirit on his preaching and he was greatly used there. His profound experience of the Lord in 1800 or 1801 encouraged Evans and rescued him from the dry and intellectual approach of Sandemanianism which had influenced him for a short period.[5]

Christmas Evans continued to preach, while longing to experience more and more of the Lord's anointing on his preaching. Under his ministry, revivals broke out in Llanfachreth in 1791 and 1805; then in Brynsiencyn in 1807, when 'the Holy Spirit anointed the Word in the ministry so that people were awakened and professed faith in Christ'.[6] This was followed in the winter of 1814–15 by another revival related to his church and its branches, when a spirit of prayer fell on the church and a deep desire for revival. The clouds of heaven opened with blessing on the work; about six hundred people were added to the Baptist churches in Anglesey under Christmas Evans's care.

From the foregoing examples we have reminded ourselves that other localities and denominations in north-west Wales had also experienced revivals and authoritative, powerful preaching. So the Beddgelert revival is not an isolated example in the early period of nineteenth-century Wales. Nevertheless, the Beddgelert revival is probably unique in the degree of power known in the preaching during 1817–1822, and also in its extensive influence through much of north Wales and even in other parts of the Principality.

As the Beddgelert revival spread to other areas, 'its most prominent feature', writes Eifion Evans, 'was the power of the preaching. What had been previously weak, ineffective, and barren was now authoritative and fruitful.'[7] And through this revival, Evans adds with justification, 'preaching regained its authority and influence in the land'.[8]

Its prominent feature

We can now begin to describe the preaching during the Beddgelert revival of 1817–22 and appreciate its power and impact.

Only a few weeks after the Hafod y Llan preaching service, when the Holy Spirit empowered an ordinary preacher like Richard Williams to deliver an unforgettable and irresistible sermon, the Rev. Ebenezer Richard (1781–1837) visited Beddgelert to preach. Brought up in Pembrokeshire, Richard had settled in Tregaron, Cardiganshire, in 1809. He laboured in south Cardiganshire alongside the more famous preacher, Ebenezer Morris, for about sixteen years, and was 'as Elisha was to Elijah'.[9] Ebenezer Richard was another useful servant of the Lord who often preached 'with demonstration of the Spirit and with power'.[10]

During his brief weekend visit to Beddgelert in 1817, Richard's preaching was powerful on the Saturday evening, and even more powerful on the Sunday morning in Hafod y Rhisgl.

As a result of his preaching, a good number of people were converted and added to the church.[11] Before the end of that year, over a hundred people had joined the church in the village—an astonishing increase!

Candidates for membership

Joining the Calvinistic Methodist church at this time, however, was neither quick nor easy. A thorough questioning and observation of candidates took place over a period of many weeks. John Jones, Glan Gwynant, provides an eyewitness account[12] of the Beddgelert revival, and he describes carefully the method used for accepting new members into the local Calvinistic Methodist church in the village.

The first step was for individuals to 'offer themselves for membership'.[13] They were then questioned about their spiritual condition before God and their spiritual experiences. After this, the questioning was directed to their beliefs. Did they believe consistently in God's Word and man's fall into sin in Adam? Had they understanding of the plan of salvation, namely, the way God planned in his grace to save man through Jesus Christ, the second Adam?

If the elders were persuaded that the Holy Spirit was at work in their lives to some degree, they then asked permission from the church for those individuals to stay in the church until there was time to converse with them further. When a suitably convenient time came, the leaders conversed with these individuals concerning their spiritual condition and their growing understanding of themselves, of God and the plan of his salvation.

If there were grounds for thinking that the Holy Spirit had started his work in them, the church was then asked to accept them to participate in the divine ordinances of God's house, namely, baptism and the Lord's Supper. If the church accepted them, their names were then written alongside others belonging to God's family. This strict procedure for receiving new church members was followed by the Calvinistic Methodists consistently during the Beddgelert revival, and for decades afterwards.

John Jones is honest in his reporting of the revival. Many of the converts persevered in grace, but among the crowds professing faith in Christ there were those who turned away from the Lord; yet 'not many'.[14] A number of revival converts also died during the revival.

January 1818

For many months the preaching continued to be powerful and fruitful. On Sunday morning 1 January 1818, William Roberts, Clynnog, preached from the words, 'A certain man had two sons' (Luke 15:11). This was the parable of the lost son and 'there was real power'[15] in this preaching service. The following Sunday 8 January at 2 p.m., Richard Williams, Brynengan, was again the preacher. His text was: 'By faith Noah, being warned of God . . .' (Hebrews 11:7).

Emphasising the danger of missing the opportunity to enter the ark of salvation, Williams spoke with exceptional authority. He later warned the congregation and began by shouting, 'You will come and ask for a place in the ark soon; but remember, careless sinner, it will be too late once it begins to rain and the great fountains of the deep open up and the gorges overflow and God will have shut inside his people in the ark.'

One of the hearers gave a heart-rending cry, 'What is this, O people?' He repeated the words under a deep sense of conviction and guilt. Next, the man jumped to the other side of the room and shouted, 'O, I see Him now.' Turning around, he went back to where he was before; then, looking extremely agitated, he tried to pray. By now the congregation was gripped by an awareness of the presence and glory of God. Some individuals were weeping, crying and praying. It was as if this man, and then others in the congregation, had first seen God as Judge before seeing themselves as guilty, lost sinners before him. But that was not the end. They understood that the Just One had taken the place of the unjust, and they could see a door of hope opening, enabling them to flee to safety for ever.[16]

The work of God's grace

John Jones again reports[17] that, for the first twelve to eighteen months of the revival, between four and nine new persons attended the midweek fellowship meeting in the church each week. The work of God's grace was so extensive in the locality that it was unlikely you could meet anyone on the road who would not talk about the revival taking place there. The effect on the local Calvinistic Church itself was remarkable, for over two hundred people were added to the membership. Although the revival made heavy demands on the church leadership, 'the Lord gave to the Elders of his house hearts to be wholly supportive of the revival and to love its success and enlargement'.[18] The church elders were also united in all aspects of church life.

The outpourings of the Spirit on this church were 'very powerful and effective'. Church services often lasted for as long as six hours, and the theme of their thanksgiving was the strength of the eternal covenant, the amazing grace and love of God, and Jesus Christ crucified. Most of the people in the congregation had between three and six miles to walk each way to and from church, and on their way home they spent much of their time rejoicing, so that the valleys and rocks around them reverberated with their praises. Indeed, so powerful was the work of grace in their lives, reports John Jones, that when a man went outside his house at night he would hear some people praying, and others worshipping and praising God.[19]

It was natural, therefore, for some ministers of the gospel from north and south Wales to visit Beddgelert, even during this early period of the revival. Some of them would be on their way to or from the annual Calvinistic Methodist Association meetings in the autumn in Pwllheli, and by their preaching in Beddgelert 'the Lord gave many blessings through them to people'. Some of these preaching services were 'unforgettable'. John Jones writes:

> It seems that no one remembers in any other place such powerful workings through the means of grace; the convictions were so powerful, pricking the heart, awakening the mind, and the showers of rejoicing in salvation extensive with their effect more obvious and permanent.[20]

But 'not to us, O Lord, not to us; but to Thy name' be the praise and glory!

In later chapters we will outline the progress of the revival outside the locality. But, first of all, we shall note the powerful preaching that took place in the Associations.

11
Association preaching during revival

After the death of Daniel Rowland, Llangeitho, in 1790, many people regarded Ebenezer Morris (1769–1825) as the leader of the Calvinistic Methodists in south Wales.[1] Brought up by godly parents in Cardiganshire near Lledrod, and then Pen-ffos, Troed-yr-aur, Ebenezer Morris at the age of seventeen moved to Trecastle in Breconshire in order to work as a school-master. About two years later, in the providence of God, a preacher[2] from Morris's home area of Lledrod came to Trecastle and preached powerfully there. Through this man's preaching Ebenezer Morris was converted, and he soon became a church member. Within a short time, the nineteen-year-old youngster was encouraged to preach, and from the beginning he was recognised as a very powerful and popular preacher.

There was remarkable blessing on his ministry. In the mid-week fellowship[3] meeting at Trecastle, as many as twenty-five people sought membership in the Calvinistic Methodist church, and all of them, except one, had been dealt with by God through the preaching of Ebenezer Morris.

He also preached in the farmhouse, Troed-yr-aur, in the area of Tŵr-gwyn, Cardiganshire, where his parents lived. The sermon he preached on that occasion was again remarkable for its power and effectiveness. His father Dafydd Morris, who was himself an able preacher and an elder in Tŵr-gwyn, exclaimed with thankfulness, 'The Gospel will never die while Ebenezer my son is alive.'[4]

After a useful preaching trip to north Wales, Ebenezer settled with his parents in Tŵr-gwyn. When his father died in 1792, he became the leader of the Monthly Meeting of Calvinistic Methodist church officers in Cardiganshire, and also followed his father in leading the Tŵr-gwyn church.

In the summer of 1817, as the revival was beginning to spread in the Beddgelert area, Ebenezer Morris was preaching with remarkable power in Carmarthen in south-west Wales. His text was Psalm 90:1: 'Lord, You have been our dwelling-place in all generations.' One minister who heard the sermon refers to 'the big question' he asked repeatedly and powerfully: 'Men! Do you have a dwelling-place to go to when you will be taken into the eternal world?' The noise of that question, the minister reports, 'was an echo in his ears and heart for a long time . . . '[5]

The Bala Association in June 1818 was also an occasion of powerful preaching. Looking back on it, a young convert, Griffith Pritchard, recalls that '. . . the presence of the Lord was very evident . . . his servants were clothed with such power . . . such unction on the ministry, that thousands . . . there have never forgotten that time . . . the years of eternity cannot erase it from their memory.'[6]

The Caernarfon Association, 1818

A year later, in September 1818, Ebenezer Morris was preaching in the Caernarfon Association meetings of the Calvinistic Methodists, about twelve miles away from Beddgelert. At the time, the Beddgelert revival was at its peak and was penetrating into many areas of north Wales, and this Caernarfon Association was to prove significant and extremely fruitful.

The Association meetings were held quarterly in both north and south Wales, and in a different location each quarter. The Associations lasted for two days at least. Public services for the preaching of the gospel were held each day, 'in accordance with the well-established custom of our Connexion'.[7] Only preachers and elders from Calvinistic Methodist churches and fellowships were allowed to attend the private sessions, and 'the whole Connexion is supposed to be present by representation'.[8] Three or more private conferences were held during the Association, 'at which preachers and elders shall be present'. Business matters were normally dealt with in the 'private conference' held on the first day, when decisions and policies regarding the entire denomination were finalised.

Ebenezer Morris was attending the North Wales Association meetings both as a preacher and as chairman of the Cardiganshire Monthly Meeting. What is of further interest is that 'all matters pertaining to the district in which the Association is held shall have priority over matters that pertain to the Connexion generally'. News and detailed reports of the Beddgelert revival must have been given in the Association, both formally and informally. In addition, all the elders and preachers engaged in the Lord's work in the area, as well as throughout Wales, would have been spoken to 'respecting their experience of the work of the Holy Ghost in their souls, [and] their doctrinal knowledge of the truths of the Gospel . . . '[9]

The preachers

Alongside Ebenezer Morris, other preachers greatly used in this Association included John Elias and John Hughes, Pontrobert. Elias's text was Zechariah 4:7 (the outstanding 'Zerubbabel Sermon'), while Hughes's sermon on 1 Corinthians 16:22 was also characterised by heavenly unction and power.

Ebenezer Morris preached an unforgettable sermon there on the words of Leviticus 17:11, 'The blood makes atonement for the soul.' The preaching meetings were being held in a large field near a well-known hill called Twt-hill, only about a mile from the town centre. After announcing his text, he noticed that a lot of the hearers were being distracted and annoyed by several local gentry on horseback, who had come out of curiosity to see what was happening. As they rode their horses through the crowd, the preacher addressed them: 'Gentlemen, will you please stay quiet for a while to hear the words of the Lord? I am going to speak about the soul and about the blood which makes atonement for it; and you have souls!'

The gentry listened intently to the whole sermon, and the vast congregation hung on the preacher's every word. The only noise to be heard, apart from the singing of the birds, was the voice of Ebenezer Morris. He stressed the fact and nature of man's undying soul, the sinner's guilt and condemnation before the holy God, and the inadequacy of everything and everyone, humans and angels, to make atonement for the sinner, before declaring the fact and purpose of Christ's death and sacrifice, which alone makes atonement for sinners.

At this point in the sermon, the preacher began to raise his voice more and more loudly, repeating the words, 'this blood . . . this blood . . . this blood . . .' (in Welsh, '*y gwaed hwn*'). Many in the vast congregation came under personal conviction of sin, while others broke out into rejoicing in appreciation of Christ's work on their behalf. A great number were converted through this sermon and became members of local fellowships or societies and churches in the surrounding area of Arfon, and across the water on the nearby small island of Anglesey.

The Rev. Robert Ellis gives his own impressions of the meeting and its impact. Although Ebenezer Morris

was a prince of preachers, yet he was taken out and above himself here. His voice was natural, as it were, like a trumpet, loud, clear and melodious . . . but the shout crowned everything. He shouted one word in his text again and again and new light flashed into the feelings of the hearers with each shout.[10]

98

According to Robert Ellis, the shout was 'more the trumpet of God than of man. God was in the shout so that it seemed the graves would open and the dead would be resurrected.' Ellis reports that the preacher's voice could be heard like thunder even a mile away in the town. Whether in their homes or walking the streets, the preacher's words, 'this blood', could be heard clearly and repeatedly by the townspeople, and they also were shaken and convicted.

'A great work'

What was the impact of this sermon? It accomplished a 'great work',[11] and Ellis, in my view, establishes this fact in at least six ways.

First of all, Morris's sermon was a tremendous boost to the Calvinistic Methodist work in the town and a source of great encouragement to the believers. Secondly, and related to this, 'hundreds of sinners' were brought to salvation through the sermon. This was an occasion of extensive reaping. Thirdly, among those saved were some immoral and wicked people, thus illustrating the power of the gospel. One example is given by Ellis. Jane Prichard was a well-known prostitute in the town, and she heard the oft-repeated words of Ebenezer Morris, 'this blood', as she walked into her home. A deep conviction of sin came over her immediately and, to the amazement of local believers, she trusted in the Lord Jesus.

Fourthly, at the end of the service when Ebenezer Morris was preaching on Leviticus 17:11, the crowds left the field for the streets of Caernarfon town, rejoicing in the glorious news of the gospel and the grace of God to sinners. The effect of the sermon on them was exceptionally powerful. Fifthly, the 'great work' accomplished through the sermon is illustrated in the fact that 'it re-ignited the revival in that it proceeded even more intensely than before . . .'[12] And a final reason given by Ellis is that from this Association the revival spread to Anglesey[13] in a powerful way, affecting several parts of the island.

Some years later, the Rev. Michael Roberts, Pwllheli, related to Dr Owen Thomas his impressions of the sermon. He confirmed the power of the message and referred especially to the angelic smile on the face of Ebenezer Morris as he explained and extolled the beauty of Christ and the merits of his unique sacrifice on the cross. 'That smile', added Roberts, 'was killing.' In addition to the hundreds of ordinary people in Caernarfon on that memorable day, powerful preachers like John Elias, Michael Roberts and others were deeply affected by this sermon.

Incidentally, Michael Roberts, having heard many preachers in Association meetings and on other occasions, makes the following general comment on the various physical characteristics of their preaching:

> there were the tears in the eyes of Jones, Edeyrn; the weeping of my uncle, Robert Roberts; the shout, and especially the smile, of Ebenezer Morris, and also the look, silence and finger of John Elias. These were the things that had the greatest effect on me.[14]

The Bala Association, 1820

Almost two years later, Ebenezer Morris was preaching in the Bala Association in June 1820. For many more years the Bala Association meetings would be signally blessed by God. Owen Jones sets the scene for us at the Bala Summer Association in 1835, but many of the details apply to earlier Associations, including 1820.[15]

The preaching meetings are held in a large field called 'The Green', close to the centre of the small town of Bala. From this field, looking beyond Bala Lake in a south-westerly direction, the people can see the majestic Aran mountain, 3000 feet above sea level, while to the east the Berwyn range of mountains is in view. The streets of the little town are thronged with people making their way to The Green, many of them having travelled miles, from places like Ffestiniog, Caernarfon, Pwllheli, Dolgellau, Barmouth, Llanberis, Corwen, Llangollen, Denbigh and Flintshire. Many have walked in groups; others have travelled on horseback or horse-pulled carts. As they enter the field and mingle with the large crowd, there is a great sense of anticipation. Clearly visible at one end of the field is an elevated wooden platform covered with canvas, which is to serve as a pulpit.

The preaching service begins with a hymn, the reading of a Scripture passage and prayer taken by one of the many preachers in the congregation. Another hymn is sung before the appointed preacher announces his text and then preaches.

Ebenezer Morris's preaching

On this occasion in June 1820, it was the turn of the Rev. Ebenezer Morris to preach in the afternoon service. His text was Romans 8:17: 'if children, then heirs . . .' One man in the congregation, Daniel Jones,[16] wrote a summary of this and other sermons as he listened to the Association preachers in Bala.

Morris had two main points. The first and longer one was, 'What it means to be children to God.' Adoption into God's family is essential, as all people are by nature sinners and, consequently, children of the wrath of God. He then showed how remarkable it was that God had even preserved their physical lives as children of his wrath. God has only one eternal Son but, through mercy, sinners can be made his children. It is an amazing fact, he insisted, 'moving a sinner from under divine wrath, and his soul through faith given union with Christ and adoption into God's family to enjoy their exceedingly precious privileges'. This is possible only because of (i) the eternal love of God, 1 John 3:1, (ii) the eternal purpose of God, Ephesians 1:3-5, (iii) the redemption provided by Christ, Galatians 4:5. And the essential characteristics of all those who are his adopted children are likeness to God, love of God's family, delight in fellowship with God, and a desire to bring others into God's family.

The preacher's second main point was that 'a sublime privilege belongs to God's children, namely, an inheritance'. There are many here, Morris observed, who could never gather as much as £5 for themselves, and some who fail to obtain enough daily food for themselves and their families; yet without hesitation they can say they have an inheritance 'incorruptible and undefiled, reserved in heaven' (1 Peter 1:3-4). This inheritance will remain the same throughout eternity, and it is more glorious than anything else in this world.[17]

The sermon was well received and effective. Again on this occasion Ebenezer Morris was aware of some gentry near the platform who seemed to have come only out of curiosity. During his message, the preacher shouted authoritatively, 'I do not want the Gentlemen there to think there are no other gentlemen but them. All the children of God are heirs, and God's children are the heirs.'[18] He shouted the words several times in English and Welsh for emphasis.

Propitiation and faith

The next day at 10 a.m., Ebenezer Morris was the appointed preacher again, taking as his text Romans 3 verse 25: 'whom God hath set forth to be a propitiation through faith in his blood' (AV). Once more we are indebted to Daniel Jones for his summary[19] of this sermon. 'The path for the sinner to have a part in the great salvation which is in Christ is "through faith in his blood".'[20] That is the opening sentence in Daniel Jones's summary of the sermon. The preacher went on to emphasise the impossibility of sinners justifying themselves before the holy God. They are guilty and exposed to everlasting death.

Morris then explained how sinners can be right with God, concentrating on the words, 'He whom God has set forth to be a propitiation'. There is not a more important word in God's book than this. How is there redemption for sinners? Only through the propitiation; and the preacher re-emphasised the word 'propitiation' twice before challenging his hearers. 'Propitiation is not mentioned in hell; therefore appreciate the proclamation of propitiation while you are still in this world.'

But what does the word mean? Morris defined it in terms both of reconciliation and also of the mercy-seat, which was the lid of the Ark of the Covenant in which was kept God's Law. 'It is possible', he declares, 'to approach the Ark which symbolises the presence of the holy God only because of the atonement.' At this point, the preacher seemed animated:

> There is not, was not, nor will be, anyone more deserving of being in Gehenna, in the everlasting prison, bound hand and foot, than ourselves; but blessed be God's name, here is a way to have release through the atonement; and this is what is so wonderful—it is of God! And the atonement has never been of greater efficacy than tonight. Every ungodly man or woman has to come under the shadow of this propitiation or be under the stroke of divine justice for ever and ever.

He went on to comment on other words in his text—'through faith in his blood'. He touched first on the nature of true faith, insisting that intellectual assent to the doctrines is inadequate. True saving faith, he reminds us, is called in the Bible 'the faith of God's elect' and 'like precious faith'. All God's elect people receive this faith: 'as many as were ordained to eternal life believed' (Acts 13:48). When the principle of faith springs from God and is placed in the soul of a sinner in regeneration, then, adds Morris, 'light and ability are also given in the soul to enable him to know God but through a mediator and to thirst for things of infinite import and value, namely, every grace from the great treasury Jesus Christ'. Indeed, Morris insists, a person must have true faith before he sees his need or the glory of Christ and his salvation.

The preacher was concerned to explain as clearly as possible the nature of true faith:

The power that brought Christ from the dead must raise us on to the Rock of Ages; the same power which will raise our bodies at the last day from the graves, enables the believer to flee to Christ and to be at rest in him as his eternal refuge. It is God who does this . . . What is faith? It is light. What is believing? It is looking through that light in the light of the Holy Spirit where there is a way of escape. Beware of taking something similar instead of faith. Oh to have true faith!

But what is the object of saving faith? In this part of the sermon, Morris explains that the answer to this important question is found in the phrase, 'his blood'. This means

the sufferings and death of the Mediator, not faith in his blood apart from his Person, but it means his Person and sufferings; the divine nature in unity with the body and soul that suffered on the cross which gave virtue to his great sufferings so that they are of infinite value.

Asking rhetorically what it is to be found in the Mediator's sufferings, Morris replies, 'atonement. Cleansing from sin . . . "The blood of Jesus Christ his Son cleanses us from all sin" (1 John 1:7). O infinite Person! We have had a look at his greatness and the greatness of his sufferings and have proved the efficacy of his blood.' In order to avoid any possible misunderstanding, Morris continued, 'Faith in his blood' involves,

(i) discerning the infinite price paid for the atonement of our sins, (ii) the soul commending the sufferings and death of Christ as the only basis of peace with God, and (iii) the full refusal to rest in anything other than the sufferings, death and Person of the Mediator.

To conclude this famous sermon, Ebenezer Morris noted the effects of true saving faith, underlining five of them. First, saving faith 'purifies the heart . . . the owners of faith cannot live in anger and jealousy nor any other sin . . .' Secondly, true faith 'overcomes the world' and, thirdly, it 'works through love'. Interestingly, Morris uses an illustration from the Puritan Thomas Goodwin to emphasise this last point. The last two effects he noted are that 'true faith lives through the faith of the Son of God', and that it 'is useful to its possessors throughout their earthly pilgrimage and it will be so in dying for those "who through the power of God, are saved, through faith"'.

However accurately this sermon has been transcribed, translated and presented, it is impossible to convey the spiritual power, authority and blessing which accompanied these words when first preached. Yes, there was a point in the sermon, as at the Caernarfon Association, when Ebenezer Morris several times shouted the word '*iawn*' ('propitiation' or 'atonement'), and more loudly each time, emphasising the word 'with power and indescribable effectiveness', according to one eyewitness, the Rev. David Jones, Treborth:

> I never heard the like of it in power and authority before or afterwards. The great crowds of people were crying and weeping . . . and the preachers on the stage were seen moving to and fro in utter confusion, crying and rejoicing. It is impossible to describe that magnificent scene . . .[21]

Nor can the scenes be explained in terms of emotionalism or mass hysteria. Many hundreds of the hearers repented of sin, trusted in Christ, joined themselves to churches or fellowships near their homes and lived transformed lives.[22] Here indeed were the permanent effects of revival preaching.

12
Dolwyddelan:
the dawn before revival

The story is encouraging and exciting. And it illustrates the Lord's sovereign grace in saving sinners, as well as the amazing ways in which he answers his people's prayers. It is thrilling to trace the way the Beddgelert revival spread to the small village of Dolwyddelan, and this chapter provides the necessary background.

Prior to the revival, there were a few believers in this area who continued to persevere in prayer and godliness. They were longing for conversions and blessing both in their families and in their neighbourhood.

The Jones family

I want first to introduce to you the Jones family. John and Elinor Jones lived in a farmhouse called Tanycastell, situated nearly a mile from the village of Dolwyddelan on the mountain road to Blaenau Ffestiniog. For a few years, like others from the area, John had walked regularly over the mountains on Sundays, summer and winter, to the village of Llanberis. His reason for going was to hear the godly parish curate, Morgan, preach the Word. After experiencing conversion, John decided to join the young Calvinistic Methodist church in Dolwyddelan, where he became a church elder.

John Jones was a craftsman who could turn his hand to almost any practical task. He was serious and self-effacing, a wise, prayerful man. Nine children were born to the couple, four sons and five daughters. After a sudden and brief illness, John died in May 1807 at the age of forty-eight and was buried in the parish.

Throughout his Christian life, John had been an outstanding man of prayer and burdened for the conversion of his children. Just before his death, his wife and their nine young children stood around his bed at home. Addressing his discouraged wife Elinor, John said confidently:

> The Lord will support you and I know he will care for you . . . do not worry over the children. I have committed them to the Lord. They are now in his care. It has been hard on my soul for me to commit my children to the Lord . . . but I have peace that he has heard me . . . and that you will live to see these answers to prayer. The Lord will truly give grace to my children and [he emphasised again with great assurance] you will see this. The Lord has told me that he will do this. I am now calm and peaceful in thinking of leaving you in the Lord's care and reassured on your behalf that he will care for you. 'Blessed be God, who does not turn my prayers away nor keep his mercies from me.'[1]

John's death occurred twelve years before the revival in Bedd-gelert reached the village of Dolwyddelan. But his prayers were powerful and effective, as we shall see.

What about his wife Elinor? Like her husband, she had been reared in the locality. Her father, in his later years, had devoted himself extensively to private prayer and gave evidence of fearing the Lord. Her mother was a committed and godly Christian; her eight daughters, including Elinor, also became Christians, and were godly women throughout their married lives.

One daughter, Jane, was the mother of the Rev. Cadwaladr Owen, whose story will be outlined shortly. Another daughter, Margaret, married a faithful, wise preacher of the gospel, John

Williams, Dolwyddelan. Elinor was the youngest daughter, and it is clear that she longed for her own children to become Christians and live to the honour of Christ. The dying words of her husband, assuring her of the eventual conversion of their children, must have encouraged her to persevere in holding family worship, instructing the nine children in the Bible, and praying fervently for their conversion.

Their prayers were answered abundantly by the Lord, 'who is able to do exceedingly abundantly above all that we ask or think . . .' (Ephesians 3:20). All nine children were converted, and three of the sons, John, David and William, became ministers of the gospel. The last-named became a useful minister in Wisconsin, America, while John and David Jones became prominent ministers in Wales. John developed as an outstanding preacher through whom many were converted. How the children were converted, however, relates to the revival period we are describing, so we shall need to retrace our steps soon.

The Owen family

We now turn to another family in the parish, namely, Owen Cadwaladr and Jane Owen. Already we have noted Jane as one of Elinor's sisters and, therefore, an aunt to the great preacher John Jones, Tal-sarn, and also to the Rev. David Jones, Treborth.

Jane's husband, Owen, was rich and worldly, though regular in attending the local parish church. Jane herself went to the small Calvinistic Methodist church in the village, which was still in its infancy.

The Calvinistic Methodist cause

In about 1770, the first sermon by a Calvinistic Methodist exhorter was preached in the parish, near the cemetery. Because a funeral was taking place that day, a fair number of people came later to hear the preaching of William Evans, the exhorter from

Fedw-arian. Subsequently, others came to preach, among them an exhorter from Bala called Thomas Ffoulkes (stepfather to Thomas Charles's wife Sally). One Sunday in the parish church, when the incumbent was absent, the curate from Llanberis—a Rev. Morgan—preached. He was a godly man with a powerful biblical ministry, and his sermon left such a deep impression on the congregation that some of its members, like Nanws and, of course, John Jones, used to walk over the mountain to Llanberis to hear Morgan preach and receive communion.

In 1780 the Rev. David Jones, Anglican rector of Llan-gan in south Wales, preached on a weeknight in the village. This was an outstanding occasion. His text for the sermon was John 7:46, 'No man ever spoke like this Man!' He was given considerable liberty and power to exalt the Lord Jesus Christ. During the preaching, many in the congregation broke out in strong crying under conviction of sin, as well as outbursts of praise and joy for such a great salvation in Christ. Several of them, like John Williams, not only experienced conviction of sin but also saw Jesus Christ clearly that evening as the only and sufficient Saviour of sinners and, with others, praised God publicly. Here was a foretaste of the revival to come.

A small church fellowship was now formed, with about eighteen persons; meetings were held in various homes, and leaders included John Williams, John Jones and Nanws. About 1782, a chapel was built for their meetings—one of the earliest Calvinistic Methodist chapels in the Meirionnydd Monthly Meeting.[2]

Leaders

Amongst the believers in this church were some gifted, outstanding individuals with colourful personalities. John Williams was a church elder who became a useful preacher of the gospel in the county for fifty-two years. His sermons were scriptural and easily understood, and he was widely respected. Another elder was John Jones, Tanycastell, whose premature death we have already noted. John Jones, y Llan, was also an elder, a man with great zeal for the Lord. At this time, well before the Temperance Movement came to Wales, it was not considered wrong to drink beer moderately, and Jones was the landlord of a pub as well as a farmer.

An elder who also merits mention here is Evan Williams, Bertheos. He was a kind and very godly man, and one who gave generously in the building of the chapel. Despite his efforts, he was unable to read, and yet was an exceptional man of prayer. His prayers were simple and often unusual. Griffith Owen records part of one of his prayers in the church prayer meeting:

> Thank you very much, good Lord, for creating us, and for creating us as you did and not as you may have been able to create us. You could have created us all without legs or arms and what could we do then, unable to walk or work? O, Lord, you made us very *handy*[3]

—and this fact alone caused him to spend time praising the Lord.

Opening the public praying at the request of the church, Evan Williams would always begin with the words that expressed his own heart: 'Our glorious Christ, the people here have sent me to you again and I am the worst of them all . . . !' His prayers, too, always ended with the words, 'our glorious [wonderful] Christ'.

Nanws

One more person in the Calvinistic Methodist church here must be mentioned; she is usually referred to as 'Nanws Cae-du'. A colourful personality who feared no one but God, Nanws was one of the early converts who had been dealt with savingly through the open-air preaching of William Evans, Fedw-arian, when he preached on a small stone alongside the parish pub.

Nanws lived over a mile from the village of Dolwyddelan and was an active church member, involved in the building of their chapel. Because of her godly life and her gift in prayer, she was frequently invited to pray publicly in the church prayer meetings, which were often held in homes. Her personality, coupled with her deep appreciation of the grace of God in Christ, tended to make her prayers earnest and memorable. In one such meeting, a man prayed for the Great King to throw our sins 'behind our back'. This was not good enough for Nanws. When invited to lead in prayer, she eventually referred to the man's request and, speaking of God's way of forgiving sins, she said,

> The brother here was mentioning our sins being thrown behind our backs, but they will come to our sight again there. Many times we have tried this in order to forget our sins, but they kept coming back into view. But when you, Lord, throw our sins behind your back, which is wide and eternal, then they will never ever surface again from there![4]

Jane Owen

After this digression we are in a better position to appreciate the kind of people that Jane Owen, mother of Cadwaladr Owen, had fellowship with in the local Calvinistic Methodist church in Dolwyddelan. Despite the fact that her husband attended the Anglican church, Jane was committed to this group of believers. Her husband Owen rode to his church on horseback; yet he refused to allow Jane a horse to ride to her chapel two miles away. But that did not deter her either. His opposition to her eventually stopped, but after moving to another house in the locality Owen died suddenly.

Jane Owen was a strong Christian, and she was encouraged through meeting regularly with her sisters Margaret and Elinor, who were in the same church. All the sisters were extremely prayerful and godly. Jane, for example, would try and finish her housework early in order to spend as much time as possible reading the Word and praying. Alongside the house where she lived (Tŷ Croes) was the river Lledr, the largest river in the parish, which flowed in the direction of Betws-y-coed. Conveniently, on the riverbank alongside the house there were lots of large stones and small rocks, and these Jane used as her special prayer place. To this spot she would resort two or three times a day, often spending hours in prayer.

In the next chapter we will be reminded of the prayerfulness of the other sisters, a prayerfulness that they sustained to the end of their lives. Again, Jane's lifelong practice is a good example of this.

Lifelong prayer

After her son Cadwaladr's conversion and his beginning to preach, Jane wrestled with the Lord in prayer for him to be empowered in his proclamation of the gospel. Such was her perseverance in prayer and discernment of the Lord's dealings with her that she came regularly to have great assurance as to the kind of preaching service Cadwaladr had experienced—even before she heard about it from him or anyone else. Quite often, on his return on the Monday from preaching, she could describe to him accurately whether he had known a difficult or a blessed time.

Her experience had been that the degree of blessing on the preached Word always reflected her praying beforehand. If she had found great difficulty in prayer, invariably the preaching was powerless. However, if Jane had known much freedom in pleading with God, then this was evidenced in a heavenly unction on the preaching. Who can assess the influence of such praying?

Even in old age, before her son went on a preaching journey Jane would say to him, '. . . the Lord will be with you . . . and I will be with you, too, but you will be in the pulpit and I will be here in prayer'.[5]

It was to such a godly, prayerful woman that Cadwaladr Owen was born in 1793. As a child, he helped to care for the animals on the farm and also listened to gospel preaching. When only twenty years of age, he married Alice Jones, a local girl three years his junior. His brother William married Alice's sister. Jane had prayed much for the conversion of her children and she did not now have long to wait for the answer. Their conversions would take place in revival.

Two more details

There are two important facts to underline before concluding this chapter. One is that in Dolwyddelan there was also an Independent or Congregational church. Although the Calvinistic Methodist church was the first non-Anglican church to be established in the village, the Independents had also preached here occasionally since the early 1800s. For example, Azariah Shadrach, who was living in Llanrwst at the time, used to preach in Dolwyddelan occasionally, and he paid an elderly woman in order to preach from outside the door of her house.[6] Another man, Morris Jones, preached more regularly, and others also took their turn. There are no firm details concerning the date when the Independent church was established, except that this had occurred prior to the 1817–22 Beddgelert revival. It was not until 1826 that they opened their own church building.[7]

It appears that the Independent and Calvinistic Methodist churches agreed to hold a united service, when a visiting preacher would minister the Word to them. One popular tradition[8] claims that the preacher was the famous Rev. William Williams of Wern (1781–1840), an Independent whose mother was a member with the Calvinistic Methodists. Charles Evans disagrees with this tradition and gives supporting evidence for rejecting it. He says that Robert Williams, who wrote down details of the sermons preached, was quite sure that he had recorded details confirming the preacher as William Havard, not Williams of Wern. Furthermore, Robert Williams had never heard Williams of Wern preach in Dolwyddelan, and this fact was confirmed by others as well.[9]

David Jones reports that Robert Williams, Ty'n-llan, a brother of the Rev. John Williams, felt constrained to start a regular meeting for children and young people so as to teach them the doctrines of the Christian faith. These meetings, beginning early in 1817, were held mostly on Tuesday evenings, and they were an important preparation for the revival. Adults were not allowed to attend. The meetings consisted of reciting psalms and other Scripture passages, hymns, sermon points, singing, and answering questions on what they had heard and recited. The teacher also encouraged them to pray, and often as many as four children would pray publicly. David Jones, as a young teenager, was sometimes invited to close the meeting in prayer, and he would plead fervently that he and others would know the mercy of God and release from the guilt of sin. After this children's meeting had started, news reached the village that revival had broken out in Beddgelert, and some locals went to witness the revival.

The preacher's challenge

It was at this time that an important preaching meeting was held in Dolwyddelan. David Jones later recalls the preacher: 'His physical size made him stand out most in my mind. He was the tallest man I ever saw. His name was Havard.'[10] Jones refers to his 'extraordinary *hwyl*', and as he highlighted for the congregation the great mercy of God,

he shouted, yes, I can imagine hearing his shout now: 'If you, people, were only to ask the Lord to come here to save you, he would come indeed. He who was on the cross deserves all this area. Start prayer meetings from house to house, from the bottom to the top of the valley, and I guarantee that God will save for his Son's sake.'[11]

An elderly lady in the congregation, possibly Nanws, accepted the preacher's challenge to pray more, as she too longed for the Lord to save—not just people living locally, but also people throughout the country. She began to prepare for the prayer meeting to be held in her home by buying two candles in the local shop, and she kept them unused, in readiness for that meeting.

Many weeks passed by, and the old lady's expectation to host the prayer meeting had not been realised. Her decisive action was to visit the shop where she had bought the candles to enquire of John Williams what had gone wrong. 'What prayer meeting?' he responded. 'The ones that the preacher was certain about that if they were held in our homes, then the whole area would be saved!' Williams was convicted, and he shared news of the incident with other believers in the fellowship that evening. One old deacon, Griffith Jones, responded, 'Heaven's blessings be on the old lady! John Williams, we had better have a prayer meeting in her house at once.'[12] And it was a good prayer meeting, even 'a first fruits of extraordinary gatherings over the following weeks'.

We will resume this exciting story in the next chapter.

13
Dolwyddelan
in revival

In addition to the adult prayer meetings that were now being held, a significant development occurred with respect to the regular children's/youth meeting held in Dolwyddelan on Tuesday evenings. Robert Williams, who was responsible for the Tuesday meeting, now thought it appropriate to make it a more public meeting to which adults could go.

The meetings were held in the church, or in houses and farmhouses in the community. Wherever an individual or family in the locality was willing to host the prayer meeting, Robert Williams convened the meeting in that home. Wherever they were held, the meetings were crowded. Clearly people were intrigued by the newness of the meeting, and attracted also by the active participation and prayers of the children. Some of the prayers were remarkable and moving, as children between ten and fifteen years of age sounded the praises of God's grace and pleaded for forgiveness.

The Rev. David Jones, Treborth, who was one of the children at that time, looked back upon these meetings as a kind of college where he began to understand major Christian doctrines and familiarised himself with the Bible. Robert Williams's meetings had a powerful influence on him and his spiritual development.[1] 'I often think', he writes, 'that his meetings were of great profit to me; and I still have warm memories of him. His wise counsel had a solemn effect on my mind to make me embrace religion more seriously and determinedly.'[2]

David Jones reports that he was fourteen years old when the 'great revival of religion broke out in Dolwyddelan'.[3] A number of reliable sources inform us that it was in 1819 that the revival reached this village in power.[4] Although the lad was religious, sincere and zealous in his attitude to the Bible and prayer, yet early in the revival he came to a deeper experience of the Lord and a greater involvement in Christian activities. For example, he was more prepared to participate in prayer in the children's meetings when Robert Williams invited him to do so. Jones also knew inexpressible joy in the Lord and, with others, praised the Lord with great fervour.

In one prayer meeting, he was lifted on to the top of the table to pray, so that all could hear him. Almost immediately the teenage boy began to thank God for his felt presence and power amongst them. 'You have given us some drops,' he prayed, 'O give us the mighty rain.' Then in an earnest, loud and tuneful tone he continued: 'O great Lord, rend the veil, destroy the covering.' He prayed this three times, until everyone in the house shouted and jumped uncontrollably, their hearts ablaze with love and praise to God. An elderly woman testified that he 'was not in the habit of shouting and jumping', as others often did at the time. It was only when he became affected by 'the heat of Gospel love that he would sing with all his strength'.[5]

According to David Jones,

it is difficult for anyone who saw that revival [in Dolwyddelan] to ever forget it. It was very extensive and extremely powerful. Many times, I saw strong, thoughtless, even trembling and pale people paralysed with fear, then falling to the ground as if they were dead.

Jones refers to many young men living in the upper part of the parish, some of them married, who were thoughtless, rather wild and troublesome. Many of these young men went to the Monthly

Meeting of the Calvinistic Methodists in Beddgelert, not to hear the Word being preached, but rather to laugh at the way people were affected by the Word as they jumped and shouted praises to the Lord. Encouragingly, many of these men were also to be converted in the revival, and we can now illustrate how God dealt with some of them.

In the background again are the prayers and prayerful concern of godly mothers, some of whom were sisters or related in other ways. For example, Jane Owen, mother of Cadwaladr Owen, and Margaret, mother of Dafydd Owen, often prayed together. David Jones explains the family connection between them: 'one [Jane] a sister to my mother [Elinor] and the other [Margaret] my father's sister'. He adds: 'These two women would go to each other's home in turn to hold family worship'[6] and pray for their children. Sadly for these mothers, their sons Cadwaladr and Dafydd were among those wild young people of the parish whom we have just described.

Cadwaladr Owen and Dafydd Owen
It was for the purpose of making fun of the believers that Cadwaladr, Dafydd and others went to the Beddgelert Monthly Meeting when the Rev. Michael Roberts preached. The text was Isaiah 9:5. There was such a heavenly power and anointing accompanying the preaching that numbers of people in the congregation were convicted of their sin and guilt before the holy God.

Among those under conviction were Cadwaladr and Dafydd. Their long walk home was difficult and distressing, but not because of the winding mountain paths. For them, the conviction of sin was painful and overwhelming. When they arrived home, it soon became apparent to the mothers that God was dealing with their sons. They were given hot milk with pepper and sent immediately to bed, as they appeared exhausted. But when they were on their knees in prayer, the two sons broke out into weeping and groaning. Cadwaladr lived next door to his mother's house, and his wife ran hurriedly to her mother-in-law to tell her what was happening. 'Milk and pepper will not mend Cadwaladr and Dafydd tonight', was her mother-in-law's response; and immediately seeing that Dafydd's mother Margaret had arrived to see where her son was, Jane embraced her, both of them shouting excitedly over and over again, '*Diolch!*' (thanks) and '*Bendigedig!*' (wonderful, glorious).

It is unclear exactly when Cadwaladr was converted. Was it that evening? or the following Sunday evening? Possibly it was another evening when he was sitting at home deep in meditation over his spiritual condition. On this occasion he heard what seemed to be an echo in the distance shouting to him: *Barn!* (judgement). *Tragwyddoldeb!* (eternity). *Nid oes do ar ddistryw!* (there is no roof on destruction). Minutes after hearing those words while he was praying, Cadwaladr began to rejoice in the Lord's mercy, and for some hours he was completely taken up in rapturous joy and praise.

John Jones

'John, I have got news to give you!' That was the message given to the young John Jones, who was staying at the time in the neighbourhood of Llangernyw, near Llanrwst.

To fill in the background to this story, John was one of the nine children born to John and Elinor Jones, and the loss of his father at the age of forty-eight had had a profound effect upon the ten-year-old boy. A serious and religious boy, John even preached to other children. However, that early spiritual promise was not fulfilled until his late teens. Although attending church and reading the Bible regularly, his love of music and singing came into the ascendancy. Working in the quarry, he began to mix socially with some of his worldly young work colleagues.

There were indications that he was being influenced by these unbelievers, and one day, despite his mother's protests, he decided to accompany them to Llanrwst Fair.

As he left home that morning for a fair that was notorious for drunkenness and immorality, his mother wept and reminded him of his late father's faith, prayers and example: 'Don't let your father's prayers for you go wasted.' For the next hours she pleaded with God on behalf of her son and his conversion.

And God answered her prayer, at least partly. Later that day, to his mother's surprise, her son arrived home in the early afternoon. He had gone to Llanrwst, nine miles away, and had joined his friends in going into the beer house. With the beer in front of them and young ladies sitting on their knees, John began to feel distinctly uncomfortable as he thought of his mother and remembered his father's prayers. Without drinking much of the beer, he suddenly got up, walked out without any explanation and ran home as quickly as he could.

He was welcomed and given a large meal. Then he declared:

> Mother, you will never again need to try and prevent me going to the fair. I have never seen such a miserable place. What the young people call pleasure is the most mad thing I have ever seen. They are fools . . . I will never again go near it . . .[7]

Unable to contain herself for joy and weeping, his mother declared, 'Thanks to the Lord! Blessed be his name for ever!'[8] After this major incident, John Jones became more serious—he sang hymns, read the Bible often and attended church regularly, yet without making a public profession of faith.

In early winter 1818, John decided to move to a farmhouse in the neighbourhood of Llangernyw, near Llanrwst, where his married sister Mary lived. There, too, singing was one of his favourite pastimes, first in the parish church, then in the chapel as he gained a reputation in the area as a singer. About this time he had a dream, which his sister claimed had a profound influence on him. In the dream he saw his own heart being pulled out and placed in a dish. He was then comforted with the reassurance that he would be given a new heart in its place. The effect of this dream was powerful, compelling him to think continually about the gospel and his own relationship to God.

Henry Rees (whom we shall be meeting again in a later chapter) visited Llangernyw to preach. He was a young man with preaching gifts who knew the power of the Holy Spirit in his preaching. Under Rees's preaching, John Jones felt his urgent personal need of salvation. He could delay no longer and turned to Christ completely for grace and mercy. At the same time he consecrated himself and the rest of his life to preaching this glorious Saviour Jesus Christ to his people.

Strangely, Jones did not seek membership in the local Calvinistic Methodist church. One of the older men in the church wisely encouraged John to sing a hymn one evening; it was a new tune to words he had originally learnt in Dolwyddelan and taught to others. The verse reads:

> *Wel, dyma'r Cyfaill gorau gaed;*
> *Mae'n ganmil gwell na mam na thad;*
> *Ym mhob caledi ffyddlon yw:*
> *Mae'n medru maddau a chuddio bai,*
> *Ac o'i wir fodd yn trugarhau*
> *Wrth bechaduriaid gwael eu rhyw.*

(Well, here's the best Friend one could have; / A hundred thousand times better than mother or father; / Faithful in every adversity: / He's able to forgive and cover sin, / And of His own volition He shows mercy / To vile sinners.)

As he sang these words, especially the last two lines,[9] John was so deeply moved that he found it difficult to restrain his emotions and he was anxious to stop singing. However, one of the older men, Robert Dafydd, sensed what was happening and decided to continue repeating the singing of the verse until the words had truly blessed the young singer. When the singing eventually finished, John Jones fled quickly and quietly from the room into the night air. Some friends were walking in the same direction, but finding their company intrusive he eventually excused himself, and fell to his knees to seek mercy and to throw himself again into the arms of 'the best Friend one could have'.[10] Many of the details of this experience are not recorded, but one thing is certain: John Jones was greatly blessed that evening by the Lord; his new-found assurance of salvation was genuine and deep.

The exciting news

Having set this story in its context, we can now return to that Monday morning when John was told, 'I have got news to give you!' The messenger was a herdsman who had come from Dolwyddelan that morning. And the news? 'A revival has broken out in Dolwyddelan,' he reported. 'Cadwaladr Owen, your cousin, was shouting—you have not heard anything like it! And the old people of Dolwyddelan have never seen such things as happened last night.'[11]

For John Jones, the decision to go home and witness what was happening in Dolwyddelan was immediate. On his arrival he went to a singing meeting where a Christmas anthem was being sung. John's brother William was singing bass, and upon several repetitions of the word '*Ceidwad*' (Saviour), Cadwaladr rose and started shouting, '*Mi ddyweda'i Geidwad i bwy ydyw*' (I will tell you to whom he is Saviour), and they rejoiced together. John went out for a while with Cadwaladr's brother William, but he returned at about 11 p.m. to 'persuade' the Christians to be more restrained. It did not work, however; within minutes William himself was rejoicing and 'shouting as noisily as any of them'!

John Jones does not seem to have lost control of himself at all, except on one occasion when his brother David Jones had led family worship in a helpful, effective manner. Immediately after his prayer, John stood up, shouting:

> You thought, Satan, that you would have me, and actually that is what I also thought. But now I think you will be disappointed . . . you will never have me. Yes . . . the Lord Jesus is for me . . . O, thanks to him! O dear Jesus!

By now, everyone in the house was crying, and John's mother Elinor was rejoicing over the way the Lord was dealing with her children.

Richard Jones

Only one brother in the Jones family now remained unconverted. Richard was living and working a few miles away in Trefriw. In the heat of the revival he went home one Sunday for a few hours. During his brief stay he was rebuked by his brother John for swearing, and he felt that rebuke deeply. A fortnight later he returned home for the weekend and there were signs of reformation in his life.

That Sunday evening, the Lord worked savingly in Richard's life. The story is related by his brother John.[12] The four brothers shared two beds in their room in the loft; John and Richard shared a bed. As John was on his knees praying, Richard understood that he was being prayed for by his brother and this fact overwhelmed him. Weeping, shaking, and experiencing powerful conviction of sin, Richard got up and jumped along the two lofts in the house. His brothers were frightened, and their mother, hearing the noise, ran up the stairs thinking that her children were playing wild games. 'Are you playing games on Sunday night?' she asked. Her question convicted Richard even further, so he cried out, 'Oh! What shall I do? What shall I do for my life?

Oh, dear people! My life! My life! Oh, what shall I do? My soul is lost!'

There was none better than his mother Elinor to counsel and help him in his spiritual despair and estrangement from God. Using and applying the Scriptures wisely to his condition, she emphasised the glories of the gospel and the sufficiency of Jesus Christ as the Saviour of sinners who was willing to receive repenting sinners. Her words, spoken with joy to him a little later, are memorable:

> I feared greatly for you, my dear boy, but here are my prayers for you heard. Here are the many old fervent prayers of your father being answered. Many times I have thought about what he said to me just before he died, 'You will see that the Lord will give grace to my children; he has told me he will do so.' And here are his words fulfilled.

Then, speaking more specifically of her son Richard, and bearing in mind the conversion of all the other children, Elinor continued,

> All are in the house of care apart from yourself, but I now have a strong confidence about you. Blessed, blessed be God! Oh, that I could love the Lord with more enthusiasm and trust him more fully! How can I praise him adequately? Praise the Lord with me! Who can remain quiet?[13]

It was a remarkable evening. A married sister of Elinor's lived next door with her family. Hearing the noise of praise from the adjoining house, she got her family out of bed and they all joined their relatives in praising the Lord. For hours their joy was irrepressible; just to hear Elinor praising God so warmly and zealously was a blessing to them all. John Jones and his younger brothers were deeply affected, alternately laughing and weeping for joy. Quite often the boys shouted '*Bendigedig*', a word that can be translated as 'blessed' and is an expression of deep joy and praise to the Lord.

Prayers had been answered, and many families were united in the gospel—for this was not confined to the Jones or the Owen families in Dolwyddelan. Lives were transformed. Heavenly, irresistible power accompanied the preaching and reading of the Word.

In the next chapter, we will give further illustrations of revival power, and particularly its physical impact on people.

14
Revival phenomena

Before tracing in the next chapter the extending influence of the Beddgelert revival beyond Dolwyddelan to other parts of north Wales, there is one matter arising from the preceding two chapters which needs to be clarified and explained, lest it be misunderstood.

The matter concerns the rejoicing of Christians in revival, a rejoicing which often led spontaneously to shouts of praise, uncontrolled weeping and even 'jumping'. Such phenomena have frequently been dismissed as inappropriate and explained away as unnecessary, and nothing but emotionalism. And Christian leaders in the eighteenth and nineteenth centuries were severely criticised for tolerating or even encouraging such behaviour. The criticism is a serious one and it is necessary to make some observations in this connection.

A feature of revivals
The first observation is that these phenomena actually occurred during periods of revival in Wales, and particularly under the powerful preaching of the gospel. However uncomfortable we may feel about it, the phenomena were a feature of the revivals. Dr D. Martyn Lloyd-Jones, for example, confirms that

> there was often great shouting during the preaching. They would interrupt the preacher, they would cry out their 'Amens' and 'Hallelujahs', and sometimes the excitement was quite marked. This joy and rejoicing and singing and assurance were the great characteristics of Welsh Calvinistic Methodism.[1]

Not new

A second observation is that these phenomena were not something new to Wales when they first occurred in the areas of Beddgelert and Dolwyddelan during the glorious revival of 1817–1822. Cadwaladr Owen, John Jones and other local believers were only representative of others in north Wales who experienced such phenomena during this revival. However, one needs to go back some eighty years or more to the early years of Calvinistic Methodism to read of the first expressions of such joy in Wales.

Earlier examples

Tudur Jones refers, for example, to John Williams (1757–1839), Dolwyddelan, who speaks of reaching Llangeitho exhausted after walking the entire distance of nearly one hundred miles from his home in Dolwyddelan. His purpose in walking so far was to hear Daniel Rowland preach. When Rowland started preaching, Williams says that in his preaching he was 'tapping the barrels of the covenant of grace' and throwing wine on the congregation. The language, of course, is metaphorical but refers to the power of the preaching and the spiritual benefits which the people derived from it. 'I drank of it,' reports Williams, 'until I was drunk like a fool; and that was where I was, and scores of people with me, without thinking of tiredness, shouting, and some of us jumping, for hours.'[2]

Tudur Jones refers to other well-known examples of shouting and jumping. Dafydd Morris (1744–1791) preached in the Llanllyfni Association in September 1779, and Christians present jumped repeatedly for sheer joy because of the gospel message.

Catherine Prichard, Llanllyfni, is reported to have had a special blessing under the preaching of the evangelical curate Richard Nanney (1691–1767), and she was the first among the

Methodists in the county of Caernarfon to jump in praising her God. Many others in the area followed her example.

During the 1785 revival in Brynengan, a Margaret Evans warned the 'angelic' preacher, Robert Roberts, Clynnog, 'to stop shouting so much and beware of killing himself in jumping!' When John Elias preached in Bathafarn in about 1796, William Jones, Dôl-y-fonddu, was 'shouting and jumping like a boy!' There were occasions when Elias was unhappy with such expressions of rejoicing, and in Bala in 1807 he stopped these expressions of joy and praise.

On 27 May 1806, Thomas Edwards preached at the opening of a new church building in Bedford Street, Liverpool, but at times in the sermon he too was jumping like other members of the congregation. One famous area for these phenomena was Troedrhiwdalar. Such was the blessing experienced under exceptionally powerful preaching that the people of Builth Wells referred to the Christians there as 'the jumpers of Troedrhiwdalar'. The practice was known in Crug-y-bar too, where Nancy Jones was renowned for her rejoicing. Congregational and Baptist churches knew the phenomena in addition to Calvinistic Methodists, although it was more prevalent amongst the latter, particularly in the early period.

A historian's comments

A third observation is now appropriate, namely, that criticisms of the phenomena were taken seriously and there was no attempt by preachers or church leaders to exploit feelings and create excitement leading to shouting and jumping. I confine myself at this point to the example of a Welsh Calvinistic Methodist minister and historian, William Williams (1817–1900).

In his book, *Welsh Calvinistic Methodism*, Williams provides a useful and 'semi-polemical'[3] history of the Presbyterian Church of Wales. Williams pastored a Calvinistic Methodist church in

Swansea for many years and proved himself a competent preacher and author. In a chapter dealing with the history of revivals in his denomination, Williams is only too aware of critics who dismiss revivals as consisting of 'all excitement'.[4] His defence of revivals, and especially the phenomena of shouting and jumping, is interesting and helpful.

He acknowledges, first, that 'there was excitement . . . and much of it . . . But to say that it was all excitement is quite another matter . . .' If by 'excitement' a 'momentary feeling' is meant, one which lacked any 'lasting beneficial effect' on people who experienced it, then Williams rightly insists that there is 'abundant and conclusive evidence in thousands of instances'[5] that the critics are wrong. Many thousands of people who witnessed or experienced the phenomena had their lives transformed permanently in such times of revival.

Williams is clearly reluctant to defend all that happened in the excitement, but he nevertheless insists:

> it is certain that thousands of those who were thus excited, and who expressed their feelings in cries of distress, and in shouts of gratitude, underwent at the time the great change, and proved themselves for the remainder of their lives to be new creatures.[6]

Did the preachers encourage and produce such manifestations? That is the question that Williams addresses next. 'Some excellent men', he writes, 'seem to have been under the impression that the preacher had only to say "Shout" and that the people shouted, and to say "Jump" and that they jumped accordingly.' In language that is unambiguous and frank, Williams dismisses this as 'an absurd caricature'.[7] But were such phenomena regarded by the early Welsh Calvinistic Methodist leaders as 'necessary accompaniments of true religion'? The answer is a negative one; but Williams, without pursuing the question in detail, here raises a crucial subject, and it is one which has continued to trouble churches until the present day.

Not essential

A fourth observation can be made on this subject, namely, that the God-centred, biblical theology embraced and taught by the Calvinistic Methodists at this time prevented them from encouraging emotionalism and physical phenomena. To put it more strongly and theologically, they did not regard such phenomena as being essential to a true work of God.

I want to illustrate this point by referring to a more famous William Williams (1717–1791), of Pantycelyn. This gifted Christian 'wrote nearly a thousand hymns, travelled over a hundred thousand miles while preaching, and wrote more than ninety books'.[8] He wrote some letters, elegies and hymns in English, but most of his literary work was in Welsh. His works were so useful to his contemporaries and to later generations that Eifion Evans suggests that 'he could be fairly thought of as a Welsh Charles Wesley and Jonathan Edwards rolled into one'.[9]

Converted in revival and participating in several revivals during his ministry, Williams became an Anglican clergyman. Later, from 1743, he assisted the Rev. Daniel Rowland in Llangeitho, where there was much blessing on the work.

The year 1764 saw the publication for the first time of Williams's *Life and Death of Theomemphus*. This original work was in Welsh, but in metre and rhyme, extending to 1,451 verses. His aim in writing it was to provide, in poetic form, a theology of Christian experience which was thoroughly biblical, balanced and experimental. For many generations of Welsh-speaking Christians, the book became a religious classic and a key text of theology and counselling. The major emphasis of the work is 'the inadequacy of a Christianity which stops short of heart-religion'.[10]

It must be underlined that the theological framework employed by Williams was thoroughly Calvinistic and biblical. The Bible, for example, is God's written Word, the only source of truth and the sole authority for belief and practice. God is sovereign in planning, then accomplishing, salvation through the unique, substitutionary death of Christ. But even the application of salvation to an individual is the omnipotent and sovereign work of God. Only the Holy Spirit can bring spiritual life to people, people who are spiritually dead in sins, and rebels as well as enemies of God. It is the same Holy Spirit who indwells, keeps and strengthens believers, producing the fruit of righteousness in their lives.

Eifion Evans, in his helpful introduction to *Theomemphus*, puts this in context for us:

> Williams lived and ministered in a time of great spiritual activity. Thousands were coming to faith in Christ, claiming to be converted, aspiring to elevated spiritual experiences. Some were being added to the churches, only to fall away in time, showing their profession to have been suspect, and their 'conversions' perhaps spurious. Williams therefore deals at some length with the work of conversion, and shows us what is involved . . . There must be the accompanying ministry of God's Spirit, making the truth come alive to the mind and heart, applying it individually and powerfully, enabling a personal, believing response. Only then has the sinner started to journey to glory.[11]

The implication of these truths for preaching was clear to Williams. God uses the preaching of the Word as the normal instrument and means for bringing the elect to Christ. Fervency, urgency, but especially divine power, should characterise the preaching of the gospel; yet we must not, according to Williams, try to rush or pressurise people into making decisions. Evans warns us:

we are all too easily intimidated into using methods which are psychologically fruitful but spiritually disastrous. Faced with these pressures, Williams counsels caution, and *Theomemphus* provides us with an example of valid preaching and sound pastoral care.[12]

Similarly for Williams, profound spiritual experiences and their inevitable expression on occasions in physical phenomena must proceed 'not from the excitement of emotionalism, but from a real knowledge and enjoyment of God'[13] which results in spontaneous, exultant praise.

Dr Geraint Gruffydd confirms that 'the practice of jumping in response to the Word preached' was 'a practice which began in 1762'[14]; in fact, 'the singing and the jumping', he reports, 'began with the Llangeitho Revival of 1762–4'.[15]

It was William Williams of Pantycelyn who provided 'the earliest' of the defences of this phenomenon, and he did so in two valuable pamphlets. The first, written in Welsh in 1762, was given a long title:

> *The letter of Martha Philopur to the Reverend Philo Evangelius her Teacher. Relating to him her experience and those texts of Scripture which came to her memory, to confirm that wonderful and strange work of the Lord's which appeared upon the souls of multitudes of people in Cardiganshire, and which is now spreading abroad into neighbouring churches.*[16]

A year later, in 1763, the second pamphlet was published, again in Welsh, this time with a briefer title, *The Reply of Philo-Evangelius to Martha Philopur*. (With reference to the former we shall use the abbreviation *LMP* (*Letter of Martha Philopur*), and to the latter, *Reply*.)

One major point that is made is that a genuine work of God is often mixed, partly because of Satan's wiles, and also because of the dominance of natural passions over the spiritual in believers. However, this 'commixture' does not invalidate the work of God.

In an attempt to justify rationally the phenomenon of singing and jumping in response to gospel preaching, the following points are made by William Williams and are summarised by Dr Geraint Gruffydd:

> it is natural for lovers to praise their loved ones; it is fitting that our bodies, including our tongues, should be at God's service; it is fitting that we should be bold in that service; and it is natural, since emotions affect bodily actions, that 'people who are full of the love of God should sing, praise, leap for joy, laugh aloud and sound out praise to God'.[17]

Williams then turns to consider the evidence of Scripture and church history, before referring to those who rejected the singing and jumping associated with the 1762 revival in Llangeitho:

> their religion is in their understanding only, and has never ascended into their hearts . . . With the heart man believes unto righteousness; that men have believed some form of doctrine, however true that may be, if the principles which he has received with his understanding have not become rooted in his heart, so that he loves the Son of God, rejoices in his salvation, denies himself, takes up his cross, follows the Lamb through all his tribulations, then his knowledge only serves to puff him up.[18]

Williams Pantycelyn goes on to describe a preacher whom he calls 'Pneumaticus'. This preacher is a man filled with the Holy Spirit, and the revival phenomena of singing, jumping and prostration characterise part of the congregation's response to such powerful preaching. However, he pictures two critics in the congregation, namely, 'Formalistus' and his wife 'Florida', who are occasional visitors to the Calvinistic Methodist meetings. Extremely upset by the singing and jumping, the couple go to see the vicar and, over tea, report on the meeting and condemn the 'hypocrites' in the Methodist meeting. Later, they join the vicar in the parish church for Evening Prayer. Williams pictures the couple responding enthusiastically to the exhortation given by the vicar from the Book of Common Prayer that the people should praise God and rejoice in him, even with their hands and with shouts of joy—precisely those things they had witnessed but condemned among believers in the Methodist meeting!

Finally in this *Reply*, Philo-Evangelius emphasises that a genuine work of God in revival cannot be assessed merely in terms of outward signs. He supports the point in four ways:

First, those affected by the revival were transformed in the way they lived.

Secondly, the converts delighted in the major doctrines concerning salvation, especially the doctrine of free grace.

Thirdly, their view of the person of Christ was thoroughly biblical and orthodox.

Finally, they alone suffered persecution at that time.

The points are telling ones indeed.

Interestingly, at the end of the *Reply*, Williams translated a brief passage from the pamphlet by Jonathan Edwards, the outstanding theologian from New England, entitled *The Distinguishing Marks of a Work of the Spirit of God*, which had been first published in 1741. Williams was familiar with other works by Edwards, particularly *A Faithful Narrative of the Surprising Work of God . . .* (1736), and also with *Some Thoughts Concerning the Present Revival of Religion in New England* (1742). There is no evidence that Williams knew Edwards's other valuable work on the subject, *A Treatise Concerning Religious Affections* (1746).[19]

Williams is prepared to challenge and rebuke Christians who do not know this dimension in their Christian experience:

O Jesus, how can any, to whom you've given sight,
Forbear from singing praises and hymns both day and night?
And who can still be silent, that feel Christ's saving blood,
Its value and its virtue, to make us right with God?[20]

Critics would do well to take this rebuke to heart, and to be re-assured of the fact that the vigorous Calvinistic theology of these Welsh Methodists prevented them from promoting or exploiting emotionalism and excitement in periods of revival.

The nature of revival

A fifth observation can now be made concerning the nature of revival itself. The same Holy Spirit who regenerates, indwells and sanctifies sinners, illumines their minds constantly concerning the content of Scripture and helps them in prayer. But that is not all. There are occasions sovereignly chosen by God, when this same Holy Spirit allows greater degrees of his power upon the preached Word and, through that Word, upon believers. And this is revival.

There are three implications of this view of revival which need to be underlined before we leave the subject. The first is that while great numbers of people are converted in seasons of revival, the term 'revival' refers primarily to Christians, and to a spiritual enlivening and quickening in their own Christian experience.

Williams of Pantycelyn provides a helpful illustration of this principle. He gives an imaginary account of an experience meeting with a small number of discouraged Christians, whose spiritual condition he describes as being 'cold' and in 'dire straits'. The Christians were planning to stop meeting, so it was a desperate situation. Williams takes up the story:

We were about to offer a final prayer, fully intending never again to meet thus in fellowship . . . with the door shut on every hope of success, God Himself entered into our midst, and the light of day from on high dawned upon us; for one of the brethren—yes, the most timid of us all, the one who was strongest in his belief that God would never visit us—while in prayer, was stirred in his spirit and laid hold powerfully on heaven, as one who would never let go . . . The fire took hold of others—all were awakened, the coldest to the most heedless took hold and were warmed . . .

This sound went forth and was spread from parish to parish and from village to village . . . Now the tone of the whole district was changed . . .

Today, nothing counts but Christ, and He is all in all.[21]

Here are the essential ingredients of a God-given revival: believers being 'stirred', 'awakened', 'warmed', and Christ being 'all in all' to them. 'Restoration and effusion' are the words used by Evans to describe the biblical teaching on revival. And the words are appropriate, for they describe what happens to Christians at such times.

The second implication of this doctrine of revival is that, so extensive and intensive were the effusion and power of the Holy Spirit in revival that physical phenomena on occasions were inevitable. The Spirit's irresistible power in applying the Word to the minds and consciences of individuals was compared by Williams to 'sunrise after a cold, long, dark night' or to a 'summer's day' in contrast to winter. The shouting and jumping for joy resulted from a real, intense and profound view and experience of God. This is what evoked such outbursts of praise and joy.

In *LMP* (1762) Martha Philopur says challengingly:

The earliest opportunity I get, while Christ's love burns within me, and I give vent to my spiritual emotions, it is inevitable that

I shout the Lord's praises; I bless and magnify God; I leap and shout for joy, in so great salvation . . . At such times my memory is more alert, and innumerable Scriptures flood into my mind, all of this one theme—praising God for his free grace.[22]

The glories and wonders of God's grace to sinners in Christ evoked such a deep spiritual response and appreciation from individuals that they could not but express their immense joy in shouting and jumping.

The third implication of this doctrine of revival is that Christians in eighteenth- and nineteenth-century Wales did not encourage such excitement and phenomena. Christian conversion involves emotion, but it cannot be reduced to mere emotion. Genuine conversion involves the whole person. Gospel truth, for example, is addressed to the mind and conscience in the first place. Under the blessing of God, gospel truth then involves the will and affections. In this profound spiritual change the whole person is involved.

Similarly, in periods of revival there is a far greater degree of the Spirit's power at work upon the Word. And this issues in a felt sense of God's presence, intimate communion with the Lord, and a sense of amazement coupled with love, joy, zeal and holiness.

Consequently, there are no special means or methods required in order to obtain or promote revival. The 'great means' are especially the preached Word of God and prayer, but emotion is not one of these 'great means'. It is the Holy Spirit who makes these same means of the Word and prayer more effective at certain times than on other occasions. But physical phenomena like jumping and shouting do not belong to the essence of revival. Such phenomena cannot be identified with spiritual experiences.

To summarise

We are now in a position to summarise our discussion in this chapter. The physical phenomena like shouting and jumping have now been considered in their theological and historical context. There was no attempt on the part of church leaders in Wales in the eighteenth and nineteenth centuries to promote these phenomena, nor did they see them as belonging to the essence of revival. They would clearly have rejected contemporary movements like the 'Toronto' blessing, which encouraged and gave prominence to physical phenomena like laughter and being 'slain'. For these earlier church leaders in Wales, physical phenomena were viewed as unimportant and occasional, though part of an inevitable response by humans to the exceptionally powerful workings of the Holy Spirit in periods of revival. While William Williams of Pantycelyn and Daniel Rowland of Llangeitho and others were prepared to defend such phenomena in periods of revival, yet they had a low profile, for what captivated the hearts and minds of believers were the truths of the gospel and the wonders of saving grace.

In the next chapter we will trace the spread of the revival from Beddgelert and Dolwyddelan to other areas in north Wales.

15
Revival impacts north Wales

The Beddgelert revival, as we have seen, was primarily a preaching revival. Its 'most prominent feature'[1] was not just preaching but powerful preaching. Years later, the Rev. David Jones (1805–68) compared the major revival of 1858–60 with the Beddgelert revival of 1817–22. Concerning the former he claims, 'the great outpourings were in the prayer meetings then, and there was not much stirring seen in the preaching at all'. By contrast, he writes, in the years 1817–22 'in the sermons specifically the mightiest outpourings of the revival occurred. The ministry was greatly honoured at that time. The might accompanying the ministry of the Word cannot be described.'[2] Even seeing a preacher like the Rev. Daniel Jones getting up in the pulpit affected the people, and when he began to speak, 'the whole congregation was seen to be on fire'.

Not all will agree with Jones's assessment of the 1858–60 revival in Wales. Preaching was important in that revival; it was one that 'restored the ministry to its New Testament prestige and vigour', including 'an unmistakable reversion to the plain preaching of the saving truths of the gospel'.[3] Eifion Evans adds: 'At no time . . . were the prayer meetings allowed to replace or exclude the preaching of the Word. The experiences of the revival were thus tempered with a sound knowledge of the truth . . .'[4]

These points must be acknowledged: in relation to the 1858–60 Welsh revival, preaching was important, and it was fruitful. On the other hand, since David Jones lived through both these revivals, his testimony carries considerable weight. It is also worth remembering that the 1858–60 revival was affected by strong 'Finney' influences.

What David Jones may have had in mind, however, was that in the Beddgelert revival of 1817–22 preaching was supreme. Whether in Associations, Monthly District Meetings, local churches, homes or in the open air, preaching was in its 'golden age' and exceptionally powerful. And this was not confined to one, two or even three preachers. In addition to Richard Williams, Brynengan, there were other local preachers as well as itinerant preachers (some of them famous), such as Michael Roberts (Pwllheli), Ebenezer Morris and Ebenezer Richard, whose preaching during the revival was irresistible. In this respect it was unlike the 1858–60 revival, for between 1817 and 1822 in north-west Wales no one preacher or leader could be singled out as towering above others in the measure of heavenly anointing, power and effectiveness upon their preaching. There were many memorable and powerful preaching services, involving numerous preachers, some of whom I will refer to in the next chapter. If, then, it is these features that David Jones is highlighting, one can sympathise with him, without depreciating the role of preaching in the 1858–60 revival.

The historian William Williams of Swansea also speaks highly of the status and effectiveness of preaching in the Beddgelert revival.[5] He reminds us too, as we saw in the last chapter, that the divine power of the Holy Spirit was not confined to preaching. Rather, it 'came upon people in an unaccountable manner when alone or in company or when they were following their daily vocations, and when . . . there was nothing to induce them'.[6] We have seen examples of this in preceding chapters.

Wider effects

Our task now is to indicate some of the ways in which the

Beddgelert revival extended beyond the locality, and beyond Dolwyddelan, to other areas of north-west Wales. Its effect on church life in north Wales was profound and extensive. Like a forest fire, it spread quickly throughout north-west Wales, Anglesey and Denbighshire. Edward Parry, a Welsh Baptist historian, remarks:

> You would think here that the Holy Spirit is denominational in his influences, but it is sufficiently obvious that this respected denomination [*Calvinistic Methodists!*] existed predominantly in this part of the country. The great Beddgelert revival considerably strengthened this denomination—adding thousands to its churches through the country. Undoubtedly the strength and position of the Calvinistic Methodist church in Arfon and Meirion today is due chiefly to the effects of this revival. This great revival wave was a great uplift to religion in north Wales.[7]

Edward Thomas confirms the point: 'this revival was a great renewal of strength to the [Calvinistic Methodist] Connexion, because thousands of people were added to the churches throughout the country.'[8]

How did the revival spread in north Wales? Well, it did so in several ways.

Visitors to Beddgelert . . .

One obvious way was that many people from other villages and towns in north Wales visited Beddgelert to hear revival preaching and witness first-hand what God was doing. Once revival had broken out in 1817, 'Beddgelert', writes Eifion Evans, 'was visited by large numbers of people'.[9] William Williams is not exaggerating when he claims that many of these visitors 'caught the fire' themselves 'and took it home with them'.[10] Cadwaladr Owen, Dolwyddelan, is only one of many examples.

It is impossible to estimate the numbers of people who visited the revival scene during those years. What is clear is that many of them were converted or revived, and then went home to enrich their local churches or even to plant new churches. One example is the Calvinistic Methodist church in Rhyd-ddu, only four miles away in the direction of Caernarfon. The Beddgelert revival gave tremendous impetus to the work of the gospel here, and a church building was eventually established in 1825.

. . . from near and far

People travelled to Beddgelert from England as well as from various parts of Wales. One godly man from England, for example, visited Caernarfon with the desire to hear powerful preaching. Being informed there of the revival in progress at Beddgelert, he decided to travel the thirteen or so miles to the village.

While in Beddgelert, he talked to many people about the revival. One of those to whom he spoke was himself a visitor, but from nearby Anglesey. The Englishman sought an explanation of what was happening. 'The people are sorrowing and weeping and also rejoicing in the same minute', he was told. And the Anglesey visitor added that the sorrowing and rejoicing were the work of the Holy Spirit, convicting individuals powerfully of their guilt and lostness, then comforting them in the grace and forgiveness of the gospel.[11]

As we saw earlier, others who visited were more local. The revival spread quickly to the town of Caernarfon, probably prior to the famous June 1818 Association meetings in the town. As a teenager there, for example, Robert Owen (later to be a minister in London) was one of several young men in 'the Old Chapel' (*yr Hen Gapel*)—Capel Penrallt in Caernarfon—to be deeply influenced by the Beddgelert revival. There were some weeks when this group of godly young men stayed in their chapel for hours after the Sunday evening preaching service. They were described on these occasions as 'like being in a trance of love', 'rejoicing' with people 'gathering around them, listening in joy and tears'.[12]

From villages near and far, especially in north Wales, people made their way to Beddgelert during those revival years. Their motives were sometimes mixed: some went to ridicule, others out of curiosity or a genuine desire to be saved, and yet others as believers eager to experience the Lord's presence in revival.

Pennant

Apart from the visitors to Beddgelert who helped to spread the revival, the Beddgelert Christians themselves felt a deep concern for the spiritual state of nearby villages. As one example of this, the local converts in Beddgelert were going to the village of Pennant, some miles away, in order to hold a prayer meeting for the people of Pennant. The village had a reputation for ungodliness, and at this time only three people there were known to be Christians. All three were women who continued faithfully to worship the Lord in what was to them a discouraging situation.

One of these ladies, Mrs Elen Williams, refers to a group of converts walking over the mountain from the direction of Beddgelert and, as they walked, singing the praises of God vigorously and joyfully. It was the Sabbath day and it was not long before the fear of God pervaded the village of Pennant. There was fervent prayer, too, for conversions among the local inhabitants, for that was why the Beddgelert group had come.

Against the background of these prayer meetings, the Rev. Michael Roberts, Pwllheli, preached in the village of Pennant on Easter Monday 1819. His text was Psalm 1, verse 5: 'Therefore the ungodly shall not stand in the judgment, nor sinners in the congregation of the righteous.' For most people present, it was an unforgettable and mighty sermon: the awful condition of unbelievers in the Judgement Day and the awesome majesty of the Judge himself were made so real that it seemed as if they were actually present. Prayers were answered. Nearly all in the congregation were deeply affected by the powerful ministry of the Word, and many were converted. Pennant soon became one of the most godly villages in the whole of Wales.

Walking to Association meetings

Not only did the Beddgelert converts go to villages like Pennant in order to pray; they also walked with people from other churches to the Calvinistic Methodist Association meetings which were held regularly in the North, in places like Pwllheli, Caernarfon and Bala. As we have seen, these Associations were preaching festivals which the Lord blessed extensively at this time. Gilbert Williams exhorts us: 'We must remember the great influence the Associations had, as, for example, in Bala and Caernarfon, on individuals from different fellowships for their contribution to the increase of Calvinistic Methodism generally in the North.'[13]

John Elias describes for us a visit to the June Association at Bala when he was only eighteen years of age. He lived about four miles from Pwllheli and he knew that many serious young people from all over the Llŷn area were intending to walk the forty miles to the Association meetings in Bala. They were happy for Elias to join them. The arrangement was for them all to meet in Pwllheli, and, according to Elias, it was 'a great number'[14] of young people who congregated there and then walked to Bala.

The advantage for Elias in going with such a large group was that they knew where to stop on the way for a rest and also to hear sermons. All the conversation centred around the Bible and sermons. 'Occasionally', adds Elias, 'we sang psalms and hymns, and sometimes we rested, and one or two would engage in prayer. Then we would proceed again on our journey, singing on the way.' Elias was impressed, too, that although there were many young men and women in the crowd, he did not 'recollect seeing any wanton looks', nor hearing an idle word from anyone throughout the journey. These young people were well motivated; they were going to Bala 'expecting to meet God there'. And they were not disappointed. This Association, Elias reports, was remarkable: 'life and power was in the ministry, and heavenly dew descended on the people'.[15]

The journey home, which 'we all walked on foot all the way', was also a blessing; it 'seemed to end much too soon'. In fact, Elias was so greatly blessed on the journey in fellowship with these young, godly people that he decided to join the Calvinistic Methodists and meet with these young people often. This example highlights the fact that groups of Christians from most, if not all, of the Calvinistic Methodist churches and fellowships would meet on these occasions.

While the area Monthly Meeting could often be a useful and blessed opportunity for meeting believers from other Calvinistic Methodist churches, it was the Association meetings held over a period of three to four days which were popular at this time. The Christians from Beddgelert and Dolwyddelan would mostly walk to the spring Association meetings, then to the June meetings, almost always in Bala, or the autumn meetings in Pwllheli or Caernarfon. These last venues were the nearest and most convenient for the Beddgelert believers, while Bala was an especially popular venue.

What mattered

But it was not the location that was important, but rather the ministry of the Word in power and the felt presence of God in these places. In travelling to, and attending services in, these venues, there was ample opportunity for Christians in Beddgelert to share news of what the Lord was doing in revival amongst them. In this way, other people would have taken the burden of prayer for revival home with them, and would also be arranging to visit Beddgelert.

One further illustration relates to Griffith Roberts, who lived near the village of Llanllyfni, which is approximately midway between Caernarfon and, to the south, Porthmadog. Before his conversion Roberts was a wild, violent man. Hearing that some of his former neighbours and relatives had been converted, he went to the fellowship in Llanllyfni and also to Beddgelert to see what had happened.

Then, early one morning, he joined the people walking to Caernarfon on the Beddgelert to Caernarfon road. They were going to Caernarfon for the Association meetings that were due to commence the next morning. These folk often held prayer meetings off the main road, praising God for his amazing grace. Many of them were converts in the Beddgelert revival. Griffith Roberts reports:

> I cannot describe my feelings at the time. It was as if my blood was boiling in all my veins. I could do nothing better than go into the middle of them to rejoice and praise with them . . . At the toll-house, there was a weaver living. When I was going past, he put his spindle away and came with us![16]

And such people would not have been disappointed. For example, at the end of the September 1818 Association in Caernarfon, many young people and others returned to their villages saying, 'We have had at least one Llangeitho in Caernarfon.' This was a reference to the powerful revivals which had occurred under Daniel Rowland's ministry in Llangeitho and indicates the degree of power known in this later period of 1817–22.

Preachers

If we wish to understand more fully the spread of the Beddgelert revival, it is important to underline one aspect of these Associations. Those who had preached in the Association meetings, as well as other ministers present, 'turned from Caernarfon to go to other places in the area around, including Anglesey, like clouds full of water',[17] ready to drench the villages and towns with divine grace, as the Lord would use their preaching in the surrounding areas.

But there was more too. Some of the revival converts themselves, men like John Jones, David Jones and Cadwaladr Owen, became useful, and even powerful, preachers of the gospel for years to come. This is the theme of our next two chapters—tracing more of these preachers during the revival period, and also some of the young men who were called to preach during that revival.

16
'Keeping the fire going'

Chapter 11 focused on a 'mighty preacher' who, after Daniel Rowland's time, came to be regarded by many as the leader of the Calvinistic Methodists in south Wales.

Ebenezer Morris

During the period of the Beddgelert revival, in about 1819, Ebenezer Morris was preaching in the small town of Lampeter in Cardiganshire. The occasion was the Monthly District Meeting for leaders of Calvinistic Methodist churches and fellowships in that vicinity. His text was Hebrews 8, verses 1-2: '. . . We have such a High Priest, who is seated at the right hand of the throne of the Majesty in the heavens, a Minister of the sanctuary and of the true tabernacle which the Lord erected, and not man.'

During the sermon, the preacher referred to Aaron's work as high priest in lighting the lamps in the sanctuary, and the work of the priests in keeping the 'holy' fire alight continually. As part of his application, Morris challenged his congregation: 'I expect some here are ready to say—"the old preachers had more fire than you have, and if we lost you too, then we do not know where to get others as good as you after your days".' He continued:

Ha! If that is worrying you, tell the Minister of the sanctuary; yes, tell the great High Priest who is enthroned at the right hand of the throne of majesty. It is He who cares for the holy fire and He alone lights the lamps of the sanctuary. And it is neither learning nor gifts that can light the lamp for your church sanctuary.[1]

At this point the preacher paused and, after a brief but tense silence, exclaimed: 'Our great High Priest! Let him come to light the lamps again in our churches. Keeping the fire going is his responsibility and his work alone—ask him in prayer!'[2]

Ebenezer Morris had identified one of the concerns of Christians in this period. Their best preachers were ageing and would soon be in glory, or had already gone to be with the Lord. How would churches cope in the future without such men as Morris—one who had travelled extensively, and for prolonged periods, proclaiming the gospel throughout the Principality?

Aware that death was imminent, Ebenezer Morris explained, 'My greatest desire now is that I may depart and be with Christ.'[3] He died in great peace, trusting in the Lord Jesus Christ. His death in 1825 represented a massive loss for Calvinistic Methodist churches in Wales.

Ebenezer Richard

Rev. Ebenezer Richard (1781–1837) of Tregaron was a close neighbour and colleague of Ebenezer Morris in Cardiganshire.[4] Richard had preached in Beddgelert early in the revival under the unction and power of the Holy Spirit. Many people in all areas of Wales flocked to hear him preach and 'he was eminently successful in winning souls to the Saviour'.[5] He survived Morris by twelve years.

Ebenezer Richard was born in Pembrokeshire. His father, Henry Richard, had been a circulating schoolmaster and a Calvinistic Methodist preacher for as many as sixty years. In 1801, during a period when he was himself a schoolmaster, Ebenezer experienced deep conviction of sin and a powerful conversion to Christ. A year later he began preaching. In 1806 he was appointed private tutor to a family in Cardigan, and three years later he married and settled in his wife's home in Tregaron. Only two years after his marriage, he was ordained to the Calvinistic Methodist ministry at the first ordination at the Llandeilo Association in 1811.

While he was a very powerful preacher, he was also an outstanding organiser, and served for years as secretary to the Cardiganshire Monthly Meeting and the South Wales Association. He was also the chief supporter of the Sunday school movement in south Wales.[6]

Evan Richardson

Another preacher mentioned earlier[7] is Rev. Evan Richardson (1758–1824), who had close links with Beddgelert and had preached there even prior to 1817. Born in Cardiganshire, about five miles from Aberystwyth, he was educated in Ystradmeurig as his parents wanted him to become an Anglican clergyman. Because of his deep sense of spiritual concern he discontinued his studies, and then left home, partly on account of his father's anger at his decision not to continue preparing for the Anglican ministry. He was helped spiritually both before and after his conversion by a number of Calvinistic Methodists. He also had opportunity to go regularly to hear Daniel Rowland preaching in Llangeitho, and especially on Communion Sundays.

Preacher and schoolmaster

One of the evangelical clergymen in his locality invited Evan to accompany him on a preaching tour of north Wales. The companionship was of mutual help, and the young man usually led the services before the clergyman preached. On the way home, Evan was encouraged to preach, and he did this for the first time, possibly in Dolgellau.

As a result of this trip, Evan was persuaded to become a schoolmaster in Brynengan, where his work was successful. Further moves saw him as schoolmaster, with varying degrees of success, in Pwllheli, Llangybi and then back at Brynengan, until the Caernarvonshire Monthly Meeting of the Calvinistic Methodists persuaded him to settle in Caernarfon and keep school there. This Monthly Meeting also chose him to be ordained in the first ordination of Calvinistic Methodist preachers in the Bala Association, June 1811.

His ordination was a recognition of his gifts and labours; he was certainly prominent in north-west Wales amongst Calvinistic Methodist preachers. While not an outstanding preacher, he often preached with the unction of the Holy Spirit, and churches were always eager to welcome him to their locality. He preached the gospel regularly in different parts of Caernarfon town, sometimes two or three times in an evening.

His main task in Caernarfon was that of schoolmaster, and he had the privilege of educating the preachers of north Wales and other young people who desired learning. The school was popular and its spiritual impact on the young people through their teacher was considerable. His school work in Caernarfon prevented him from undertaking prolonged preaching itineraries, though he attended the Association meetings in the North and sometimes preached in south Wales during the vacations.

Richardson's preaching was never long but always direct, expository and Christ-centred; often his hearers were aware of a heavenly, irresistible power accompanying his ministry. In his last years, when physically weak, 'he was sometimes clothed with great power when he would address a congregation'.[8] His death in 1824 represented another major loss for Calvinistic Methodist churches in north Wales. Could such a man be replaced?

To add to the concern of churches regarding the future, some outstanding leaders and preachers had died not long before Ebenezer Morris's sermon in 1819, including Thomas Charles in 1814 and John Evans, Bala, in 1817.

Thomas Charles

Charles was born in 1755 near St Clears in Carmarthenshire. He had heard the gospel frequently in his youth, but was converted through the preaching of the Rev. Daniel Rowland, Llangeitho, from the words of Hebrews 4:15—'For we do not have a High Priest who cannot sympathize with our weaknesses, but was in all points tempted as we are, yet without sin.' Reflecting on this important occasion, Thomas Charles records: 'the change which a blind man who receives his sight experiences does not exceed the change I experienced at that time in my mind'.[9] Readily acknowledging that Rowland's ministry had been the means of bringing him to Christ, Charles said of him:

I love him dearly and honour him as my father in Christ, and not without reason, for to him, under God, I am indebted for whatever light I have, and experience I have, of the glorious salvation through Christ.[10]

After graduating at Oxford University, he served several churches as an ordained curate of the Church of England. These curacies were in England and in north Wales; in several of these churches there was opposition to his gospel ministry and he was forced to leave. His burden and efforts to reach people with the gospel of grace were encouraged by the Calvinistic Methodists in the small town of Bala. Their chapel building was made available to him for instructing young people in the Bible and catechising them. From 1783, after marrying a local lady who kept a shop in order to support his work, he settled in Bala and in 1784 joined the Calvinistic Methodists.

The decision to engage in a wider ministry was not taken hurriedly. A long period of seeking advice, even from evangelical clergymen in England like Rev. John Newton, left him undecided, until he was persuaded that providentially he was being led to minister the Word outside the Established Church and to identify himself with the Calvinistic Methodists.

Daniel Rowland saw Charles as 'a gift from the Lord to north Wales',[11] as there was barely a handful of clergymen serving in the North at this time who supported the Calvinistic Methodist movement. The year 1791, as Iain Murray observes, 'marked the beginning of a passing of spiritual leadership to the North and to Charles',[12] following the deaths of Rowland in 1790 and William Williams in 1791.

Part of the inscription on Charles's tombstone indicates both the nature and importance of his work:

> By his indefatigable endeavours when in London (AD 1804) to procure a supply of the Holy Scriptures for the use of his native countrymen he became the means of establishing the British and Foreign Bible Society.
>
> He was the reviver of the Welsh Circulating Charity Schools and a most active promoter of Sunday Schools both for children and adults—and North Wales (the more immediate field of his ministerial labours for 30 years) will probably retain traces of his various and strenuous exertions to preach the Kingdom of Christ till time shall be no more.

While Charles had preached in some services with extraordinary power and blessing, he excelled more as an organiser, theologian and especially an author, where his influence would extend for generations. However, his itinerant preaching and catechising ministry in the North were greatly used by God to bring adults as well as children to faith and maturity in Christ. He was sorely missed in north Wales after his death in 1814.

John Evans

The very year that the Beddgelert revival broke out, another influential Christian leader in north Wales died, namely, John Evans, Bala (1723–1817). A preacher, exhorter and counsellor, as well as a friend and supporter of Thomas Charles, Evans's ministry was extremely useful as well as extensive, and he became famous throughout Wales.[13]

Sally Jones, Thomas Charles's future wife, wrote to her beloved and reported on a sermon preached by John Evans: 'I never heard the Captain of our Salvation set out more lovely than at that time, as overcoming all for his People, Going under infinite wrath . . .' In his reply Charles gives us his own estimate of Evans as a preacher: 'I know of no one whom I could hear with more real profit and satisfaction next to the great Rowlands himself . . . '[14] No greater compliment could have been paid to Evans as a preacher; he died in 1817.

Robert Jones

Robert Jones, Rhos-lan (1745–1829) was a teacher, preacher and author. Born in the parish of Llanystumdwy in north-west Wales, his mother gave him a godly upbringing and taught him to read the Bible. He attended one of Griffith Jones's circulating schools where Thomas Gough was schoolmaster. A preaching service when he was young 'was the means of enlightening him to see his eternal lostness and hopelessness without a Saviour'.[15]

Robert Jones persuaded Bridget Bevan to reopen the circulating schools in north Wales, and he became a teacher at a number of them: Llangybi (1766), Beddgelert (1767), Capel Curig (1768), Rhuddlan (1769), Brynsiencyn (1770), Llangybi (1772-3) and Brynengan (1778).

In 1768 he began to exhort and preach among the Calvinistic Methodists; he became increasingly prominent, and preached throughout north and south Wales. His aim was always to magnify Jesus Christ as the only and gloriously sufficient Saviour for sinners. Refusing to be ordained in the first Calvinistic Methodist ordination of ministers in 1811, he nevertheless made an important contribution to the service by delivering the charge to the new ministers.

Robert Jones married in 1772 and leased a cottage in Rhos-lan, where he erected a carpenter's shop and a building large enough to be used for religious meetings. He gathered around him a strong Calvinistic Methodist society.

His literary work was also important; this included a Welsh spelling primer (1778) and a collection of hymns (1795), which proved to be the first collection of hymns used by Calvinistic Methodists in north Wales. Two other works by Jones are worthy of mention. The first, *Lleferydd yr Asyn* (1770) was a reasoned defence of the Calvinistic Methodists against their critics and persecutors. In 1820 he published his *Drych yr Amseroedd*, in which he described the Calvinistic Methodist revival in Wales and its impact. G. T. Roberts described this latter work as 'his masterpiece; the writing is terse, the descriptions are lively, and it is permeated with the fervour of the revival'.[16]

The influence of Robert Jones was considerable even beyond his preaching and literary work. For example, he helped to discourage Thomas Charles from leaving Wales in 1784, and he successfully protected the Methodist Societies in Brynengan and Dinas from Antinomian teaching. He was also instrumental in the conversion of Robert Dafydd, Brynengan, and persuaded Evan Richardson to stay in north Wales, particularly Caernarfon, as a teacher. The fact that he had prevailed on Madam Bevan to open schools again in north Wales meant that his contribution was enormous in that direction too. And behind the first ordination of Calvinistic Methodist ministers in 1811 was Robert Jones's influence in persuading Thomas Charles to agree to the principle of ordaining their own ministers.

Robert Jones was indeed the Lord's gift to the churches.

Thomas Jones

A Calvinistic Methodist minister, theologian and author, Thomas Jones (1756–1820) was born near Caerwys in Flintshire. He was one of a small group of men who, in this period, helped to extend and consolidate the Calvinistic Methodist cause in north Wales.

Gwyn Davies thinks that he 'was perhaps the greatest Welsh theologian of all time'.[17]

Early life

Thomas Jones received an excellent classical education at Caerwys and nearby Holywell. His mother's early death was felt keenly by him and contributed to his serious thoughts about God and the purpose of life. He had a tender conscience as a child, and while he became increasingly worldly in his activities, especially on the Sabbath, he also became more aware of his own sin and the fact that he deserved to go to hell. Several providences in his childhood and youth also left a deep, abiding impression upon him. At about the age of sixteen, he came to understand gospel doctrines and knew a measure of peace with God. Displeasing his father by refusing to train for the Anglican ministry, he applied to join the Calvinistic Methodists in 1772 and made his home with them for the rest of his life.

He worked as a farm labourer, but continued to read extensively, especially the Bible. Despite attending faithfully the local Calvinistic Methodist meetings, he was troubled for about seven years by doubts which robbed him of joy and liberty in the gospel. It was in a fellowship meeting one evening that the Lord began to help him, when a woman shared how she had been helped through listening to a sermon preached in the area by Daniel Rowland, Llangeitho. Through this sermon she had been lifted from the depths of darkness and given much spiritual light and peace. By late 1779 and early 1780, Thomas Jones had known similar help and blessing, resulting in a desire to preach.

This desire was fulfilled a couple of years later, when a preacher failed to arrive at the fellowship meeting and Thomas Jones was invited to give a word of exhortation. He responded by speaking from Hebrews 11 and the believers were encouraged by his message. He became a good, acceptable preacher.

In 1784 he met Thomas Charles and there developed a close friendship between the two men. This friendship brought Jones into contact with the work of the circulating schools in Wales, as well as with the wider international work of the British and Foreign Bible Society and the London Missionary Society. The two men became joint editors of *Trysorfa Ysbrydol* (*The Spiritual Treasury*) from 1799, and they also drew up the *Rules and Design of the . . . Welsh Methodists* (1801). They corresponded with each other regularly.

Thomas Jones supervised the Calvinistic Methodist societies or fellowships in Mold (1795–1804), Ruthin (1804–1806) and Denbigh (1806–1820). He married in 1795, but, sadly, his godly wife from Mold died two years later. In 1804 he remarried, and after becoming a widower for a second time, he married again in 1806.

Writer and theologian

Thomas Jones was one of the ablest and best educated[18] Calvinistic Methodist leaders in north Wales, and he was among the first to be ordained as minister by the Methodists in 1811. His literary output was considerable, including Welsh-language hymns and poetry, a Welsh martyrology, an English/Welsh dictionary and a translation of Gurnal's *The Christian in Complete Armour*. Jones's autobiography[19] is also valuable in tracing his spiritual development and understanding his struggles and varied responses to trials and situations.

One of his major contributions was to engage theologically with Arminianism, and also with some extreme Calvinistic responses to it. For example, he opposed John Elias's view that Christ's sacrifice was an exact equivalent for the sins of the elect. For Jones, such a commercial view of Christ's work was unacceptable, because the efficacy of the atonement must rather be measured in terms of the infinite value of the Person, the Lord

Jesus, who died there. Elias accepted the point. Christmas Evans, the Welsh Baptist preacher, was also criticised by Thomas Jones for similar reasons. He later, like Elias, abandoned his more commercial, mathematical concept of the atonement, but only after a great deal of acrimony.[20]

Thomas Jones died in 1820, while the Beddgelert revival was still in progress. His loss was deeply felt by Calvinistic Methodists throughout North Wales.

Our story of preachers remains incomplete. Yes, some powerful preachers had been removed from the scene by death, and from 1817 onwards their loss was being keenly felt. Other preachers, however, like Michael Roberts and John Elias, were exercising powerful preaching ministries. And just as exciting is the fact that the Beddgelert revival provided converted men, divinely called and gifted, whose preaching would be a means of great blessing to the churches over the next four decades.

The words of the Rev. Ebenezer Morris were prophetic. As the great head of the church, Christ continued to keep 'the fire going' in his church. But more of that in the next chapter.

17
A fruit of revival: preachers

A t this point two more great preachers must be noted. They are Michael Roberts and John Elias, who exercised powerful ministries both before and well beyond the period of the Beddgelert revival.

Michael Roberts

The first had links with the Beddgelert church and the 1817 revival in that area. Michael Roberts (1780–1849) was born in Llanllyfni, a village about six miles south of Caernarfon town. Roberts's parents were believers who had been converted in a local revival among the Calvinistic Methodists. His uncle was the famous preacher, Robert Roberts[1] of Clynnog, and his father, John Roberts, Llangwm, was a schoolmaster who had himself begun preaching just before Michael's birth.

Despite ill-health as a child, Michael gained a mastery of the Welsh and English languages at an early age, then learnt Latin and Greek in Caernarfon under Evan Richardson. He became a schoolmaster in numerous places before settling in Pwllheli in 1804 and joining Penmount Calvinistic Methodist Church, which had about 120 members at the time. Later, he married and fathered twelve children.

At the tender age of seventeen he began preaching. It was recognised that he had a remarkable preaching gift, and only a year later, in 1789, he was formally accepted as a preacher by the Association in Caernarfon. His reading was extensive; among his favourite authors were famous theologians of the calibre of John Owen and Jonathan Edwards. Roberts supported himself and his family as a shopkeeper; he travelled extensively as a preacher, and from 1801 to 1829 he served as secretary of the Monthly Meeting of Caernarvonshire Calvinistic Methodist Churches.

A poet and hymn writer, Michael Roberts was a capable theologian, contributing to the writing and planning of the 1823 Confession of Faith which his denomination, the Calvinistic Methodist Churches of Wales, approved. In addition to his willingness to devote himself to this latter work, his extensive theological and biblical knowledge was invaluable. Part of Roberts's contribution was his work in integrating the two major final drafts of the 1823 Confession, one each from the North and the South, in order to have one authoritative version acceptable to the entire denomination.

The preacher

It was, however, as a preacher that Michael Roberts was most well-known and loved. Goronwy Owen describes him as 'among the princes of the Scriptures in his age',[2] his speciality being the historical books of the Old Testament and the Minor Prophets. By 1839 he had read through the whole Bible[3] forty-two times. Roberts's preaching[4] was expository, contextual, doctrinal, sensitively evangelistic and usually powerful. He was ordained as a Minister of the Gospel in the Bala Association in June 1814.

There were outstanding occasions when his preaching resulted in many conversions. In Pennant in 1818, for example, Roberts preached with such power that almost all the people listening to him were won to Christ and a 'great number was saved'.[5]

Or there was the occasion of his preaching in the Association in Llanidloes, in mid-Wales, in April 1819. Disturbed by the unbelief and ridicule of local people when he arrived in the town, Roberts spent the night in prayer, imploring the Lord to be with

him as he preached next morning. His text was Psalm 1:5—
'Therefore the ungodly shall not stand in the judgement . . .' One
person reported: 'As he began to speak, it felt as if the powers of
the world to come were pressing on the congregation in an awful
manner and increasing in power and influence until the end of the
sermon.'[6] It is believed that about 1500 people were converted as
a result of this one sermon and consequently joined churches. In
fact, this sermon has been described by his contemporaries as
one most like the sermon preached by Peter in Jerusalem and
recorded in Acts chapter 2.[7]

It was Michael Roberts who had preached in Beddgelert in
the second year of the revival on the words of Isaiah 9:5.[8] That
was the occasion when cousins Cadwaladr Owen and Dafydd
Owen had walked over the mountain from Dolwyddelan to
hear him and, like other hearers, came under deep conviction
of sin.

Roberts was frequently conscious of the Lord being with him
in power in his preaching. Writing to his son John on 24 April
1832, when he was preaching in London, he reported: 'But the
Lord has given so much of his presence in the pulpit that I have
not had to ask for anything . . . Sunday night and last night, the
Lord was in this place . . .'[9]

Illness

In the mystery of divine providence, in the summer of 1834
Roberts suffered a mental illness. During his withdrawal from
public life for about thirteen years, he was hospitalised in Chester.
After recovering, he again preached in Beddgelert, this time on
the opening verse of Psalm 23. A church elder there described it
as 'a very effective sermon'.[10]

Despite his long illness, we must concur with Goronwy Owen's
estimate of Michael Roberts as one who 'made a major contribution to the history of Methodism in Llŷn and Eifionydd'.[11]

John Elias

Another outstanding preacher in this period was John Elias (1774–1841). He belongs to the second generation of Calvinistic Methodist leaders in Wales, alongside men like Thomas Charles and his brother David Charles (1762–1834), Thomas Jones of Denbigh (1756–1820), Robert Roberts of Clynnog and, of course, Michael Roberts and others.

Describing him as a 'Prince amongst Preachers',[12] Tudur Jones claims that 'among the throng of preachers' in the first twenty-five years of the nineteenth century, 'none had greater influence than John Elias'.[13] Born in 1774 near Pwllheli, and of humble origins, his education was limited, but he did spend some months at the school run by Evan Richardson in Caernarfon. It was in 1794, just after he started preaching, that the Monthly Meeting approved him as a preacher. On marrying in 1799, Elias moved to Anglesey where he lived until the end of his life.

John Elias was a tall, commanding person with penetrating eyes and a strong, piercing voice especially suited to open-air preaching, where the thousands of people in the fields could hear him without difficulty. He engaged in expository preaching, often taking his congregation through a text word by word. His gifts of oratory and imagination were well used in underlining and illustrating biblical truth, and the ordinary, uneducated people were able to understand him easily. The result was that he 'expounded [the] Gospel with inimitable power over a period of forty years. And God blessed his work in an outstanding way to the salvation of thousands'.[14]

A new generation

As men like John Elias and Michael Roberts were exercising their ministries widely, especially in north Wales, the Beddgelert revival occurred. And it was in this revival, just as in others before and after, that the Lord kept 'the fire going' in his church by converting, then calling, some young men to the preaching ministry. All of them became useful, a few of them outstanding, preachers of the gospel. The Beddgelert revival had a quantitative and qualitative impact on church growth throughout north Wales; it helped to create a Welsh literary awakening, as well as inspiring the establishment, soon afterwards, of eisteddfods and cultural and patriotic societies of Welsh speakers.[15] But one huge gift of this revival was to give a new generation of preachers to the churches.

John Jones

Among the number of young people raised up to preach as a result of the Beddgelert revival was John Jones (1797–1857). In chapters 12 and 13 we outlined his family background and conversion detail, noting that he was one of nine children. Three of the nine children, including John, became ministers of the gospel. David became a well-known and powerful preacher (David Jones, Treborth), while his brother William became a minister in Rhyd-ddu before emigrating to Wisconsin, where he was a useful preacher and pastor. John himself became a famous preacher in Wales—John Jones, Tal-sarn. Tudur Jones has described him accurately as one of the princes of the period.[16]

We pick up his story after his conversion, when he joined the fellowship meeting, probably in Dolwyddelan, in 1819. Two years later, on a Sunday evening, and without warning, a church elder asked him to preach. The meeting was held in a house called Garnedd and he preached from Romans 8:17: 'If children, then heirs—heirs of God and joint heirs with Christ . . .' There was a great degree of blessing on his ministry, and the congregation experienced spiritual warmth and joy through the Word preached.

When he was accepted by the Monthly Meeting in Bala later that year (1821), he was free to preach more widely in the area.

Over several years he was employed as a labourer, working, among other things, on the creation of the A5 road in north Wales near to Capel Curig, and then in different quarries. Later, he relocated to Tal-sarn to work in a local quarry, and he stayed there with relatives.

John Elias, who had heard John Jones preaching so impressively in Beddgelert, encouraged churches to invite the young man to their services as a preacher, and so his preaching opportunities increased. John married in May 1823; his wife soon opened a shop and, within a year, her husband was able to resign from his work in the quarry and give himself wholly to preaching. This coincided with his acceptance by the Association as a preacher in September 1824, and his ordination followed five years later. Some of his preaching tours lasted for weeks, or even as long as three or four months.

His preaching

John Jones was an extremely gifted and popular preacher. On average, he preached four times per week for eleven years from 1821 to 1832, and in later years he became even busier. Having a thorough grasp of the Bible, he was a thoughtful and original preacher. He loved to handle great Bible themes like the plan of salvation, God's love for lost sinners, the unique substitutionary death of the Lord Jesus, his resurrection and ascension, the application of salvation and the work of the Holy Spirit. Later in his ministry he emphasised what he perceived to be the neglected truth of human responsibility.

Not only was he a gifted and popular preacher, but on many occasions he was also given extraordinary power to proclaim the gospel. He preached, for example, in the June Association at Llannerch-y-medd in 1826; the congregation became subdued and broken under his powerful preaching from John 12:24. Such heavenly power was given to him regularly.

For over thirty-five years, until his death in 1857, John Jones—raised up in the revival—was a precious and fruitful gift to the churches in Wales.

Cadwaladr Owen

Another preacher given to the churches as a result of the Beddgelert revival was Cadwaladr Owen[17] (1793–1856), whose family background and conversion we have already described in chapters 12 and 13.

Soon after his conversion, and during the heat of the revival, Cadwaladr felt a strong desire to preach, and also to share the gospel personally with individuals. Teaching in Sunday school was one way that he expressed his concern, but it was probably in 1826 that he started preaching—some five years after his cousin John Jones. Another cousin, David Jones, Treborth (brother to John Jones, Tal-sarn), began preaching at the same time as Cadwaladr. Like John, both David and Cadwaladr preached their first sermon in the house named Garnedd.

Cadwaladr's preaching opportunities increased, especially after being approved by the Monthly Meeting, and in 1833 he was ordained. This young man longed to preach Christ to sinners, and while never a famous preacher, he was a very fruitful one. One of his gifts was to preach directly and effectively to unbelievers; many were brought to see their helpless, guilty state before God, and then the greatness of his love in Christ.

His preaching was often so powerful that scores of people in the congregation came under deep conviction of sin. That was the case, for example, a couple of years after his ordination, when he preached in Llanberis on Romans 1:16—'For I am not ashamed of the gospel of Christ, for it is the power of God to salvation for everyone who believes.' Such was the authority and power of his ministry that scores of people there shouted for mercy, and many of them started going to the weekly fellowship meeting.

On another occasion he preached in Tregaron, Cardiganshire, on the words of Matthew 7:24-27, and he handled the same text in nearby Llangeitho. In both places there was great rejoicing in the gospel of Christ. John 3:36 was another text he preached on while in Llangeitho, and none of the people was able to forget the text, especially the words 'the wrath of God abides on him'. People were quiet, many holding their breath as they realised both the awfulness and the reality of divine wrath for them. In a later local revival in 1837, it is possible that no preacher was more greatly used than Cadwaladr Owen.

Over a period of approximately thirty years, Owen preached Christ faithfully and was the means of bringing many folk to Christ. But we note again that it was in the Beddgelert revival that he himself was saved, then called to preach.

Henry Rees

Although not directly related to the Beddgelert revival, Henry Rees (1798–1869) must be mentioned here, and for at least two reasons. First, it was under the preaching of Henry Rees when he was a young man that John Jones, Tal-sarn, was dealt with by God. He heard Rees preaching while staying with his sister on a farm in Llangernyw, and as a result of this sermon he was deeply moved and gave himself to Christ. Rees certainly has links, therefore, with John Jones and, indirectly, with the revival spreading out from Beddgelert.

Secondly, Henry Rees deserves mention in this chapter because he is regarded by some as one of the greatest preachers ever in Wales. His brother William, known later as Gwilym Hiraethog (1802–1883), also became a preacher of the gospel, being ordained in 1831. William was a popular preacher, serving as a pastor in Denbigh (1837–43) and Liverpool (1843–75). To both brothers, preaching the Word was of supreme importance. But there were differences in their preaching styles, and in the extent as well as the nature of their preparation for preaching. Henry prepared thoroughly and wrote most of his sermons down in large paragraphs. He worked hard to develop his preaching gifts, always expressing himself with theological precision and clarity. His brother William[18] was more free in his approach and less inclined to prepare notes. Towards the end of his life, William wrote:

> I have tried my hands at many things and am a kind of Jack-of-all-trades, prose writer, poet and preacher, and am not much of either; but my brother, Henry, has stuck to one thing, viz.—preaching, and he has made his mark in it and is a master of the art.[19]

Both Henry and William were born into a godly Calvinistic Methodist family in the Llansannan area of north Wales near Abergele. Their father was a church officer, and so powerful in prayer that people often preferred to hear him pray than to listen to a famous preacher!

Their home was often visited by some of the greatly used Methodist preachers like Ebenezer Morris and John Elias. It was under the latter's ministry that Henry was greatly blessed and overpowered by the grace and power of God. In his early teens he would preach on his own in the stable, or on the hills with the sheep; then at the age of twenty he began his public preaching. He was immediately recognised as a potentially great preacher.

Pastor and preacher

In 1821 he went to Shrewsbury to learn the craft of bookbinding. But, more importantly, from 1823 he cared for the church there as pastor and preached under the anointing of the Holy Spirit. During this period he saturated himself in Puritan writings and obtained an excellent grasp of theology. Ordained in 1827, he moved to a Liverpool pastorate in 1836.

As a preacher he was outstanding and was often called to minister the Word in Associations or on other special occasions. His understanding and appreciation of the gospel were exemplary. To him, God's eternal covenant of grace was a constant source of amazement and worship. He gloried in Christ's Person, mediation and exaltation. Owen Jones confirms this point: 'He was always with Christ, the glory of His person, the purity of His life, the agony of His death, the sinner's need of the Saviour and faith in Him. These were his great truths . . .'[20] And being such a man of prayer, the Lord frequently blessed him with a heavenly anointing on his preaching, which in turn resulted in great blessing for many of his hearers.

Once again the Lord had raised up another preacher for his church.

Robert Owen

Another young man who was blessed and quickened throughout the period of the Beddgelert revival was Robert Owen (1803–1870). Brought up near Llanllyfni in the Caernarfon area, Robert was blessed with godly parents. His mother was a sister to both Robert Roberts, Clynnog, and John Roberts, Llangwm (and so, of course, an aunt to Rev. Michael Roberts, Pwllheli). The family moved to Caernarfon because of their business. It was providential that Robert spent his childhood and youth in that town; he was able to attend Evan Richardson's school in Caernarfon for several years and read extensively.

In his mid-teens, the Beddgelert revival broke out, and this was the period of his conversion. The years 1818–20 were of special importance as he fellowshipped with other young people in Pen'rallt Chapel, Caernarfon, for purposes of prayer, instruction and rejoicing in the Lord. It was one evening in one of these fellowship meetings that the Holy Spirit fell upon Robert Owen. Years later, when visiting the town in 1854, he reflected: 'Here', referring to the site of the 'Old Chapel', Penrallt, 'I saw more of God than at any time in my life.'[21] He continued: 'In the chapel in this place I saw and experienced the meaning of the words, "And in Your majesty ride prosperously because of truth, humility and righteousness; and Your right hand shall teach You awesome things" (Psalm 45:5)'—he stressed the closing words as he spoke. He was also blessed powerfully under the preaching of John Elias and saw clearly with great joy the infinite love of God as well as the glorious plan of salvation. His heart was fired with the love of Christ.

In April 1824 he decided to move to London and identified himself with the Lord's people in Jewin Crescent. A godly believer, he served as a Sunday school teacher and then an elder before being appointed and later ordained as preacher in 1858.

Robert Owen never became an outstanding preacher, but his godliness, grasp of Scripture and theology, coupled with zeal for the Lord's work, made him a useful as well as a fruitful servant of the Lord. But, again, it was during the period of the Beddgelert revival that Owen was converted, and then given by the Lord to serve the church for many years. The Lord of the church was 'keeping the fire going'.

18
The way
forward today

Revival. That has been the theme of this book. And you have now read about one regional revival in the Beddgelert area of north Wales.

Furthermore, in chapter 14 you were reminded of the essential nature of revival. It is not an evangelistic campaign or a series of 'healing' meetings. Nor is it a vast crowd of religious people or Christians meeting for 'celebration' or witness. The term 'revival', by contrast, refers to a stirring and awakening of Christians, not unbelievers. While it is true that many unbelievers are converted in revival, these conversions are as a consequence of believers themselves being awakened, and preachers ministering the Word with an unusual degree of authority. In other words, revival is the restoration of a church, or churches, to spiritual vitality and reality. At such times, the Holy Spirit works in greater power upon the Word and more extensively, initially in the church and then in the community. This is nothing less than a divine visitation in which God's felt presence is known in the church, and often in society.

On 26 October 1822, John Elias reported:

The revival goes on very delightfully in this island [Anglesey]. The kindness of the Lord towards us is wonderful. His visits and the convictions under the Word are truly powerful. Very wild and hardened sinners are alarmed and converted; multitudes are made willing in the day of Christ's power. I have had the privilege of receiving hundreds into church-communion. I received one hundred at once in a certain place; in another place fifty, in another thirty, and in another thirty, and many in several other places. Besides, other ministers have received a great many into the church. This is the Lord's doing . . .[1]

Can God do it again? Is he able and willing to do it today and in our churches? Elias's answer is a positive and emphatic one: 'God is the same with you.'[2]

Henry Rees provides biblical and theological support for Elias's answer. Rees was preaching on Joel 2:28-29 and Acts 2:16-18 under the title of 'The Pouring out of the Spirit'.

'Last days'

He makes clear that the words of the text—'in the last days'— refer to the gospel age stretching from Pentecost to the return of the Lord Jesus in glory. Rees emphasises also that this promise, given by God through Joel concerning the Holy Spirit and partially fulfilled in Acts 2, is confined to this age of the gospel.

Nevertheless, he adds that this same Holy Spirit was also present in the Old Testament church. In fact, his presence is necessary in the Old and New Covenant periods if we are to be alive to God and preserved, as well as fruitful, as believers. However, according to Acts 2:16-18 there is a special ministry of the Spirit characterising the 'last days' or the gospel age, in terms of its *extent and abundance*. And this has been possible by the death of the Lord Jesus Christ (Galatians 3:13-14).

Following this brief but important introduction, Henry Rees proceeds to answer a question: Why should we desire and expect an outpouring of the Holy Spirit?[3] He provides five answers to this crucial question, and they are answers which continue to apply today.

171

1. *The salvation of the world, in terms of its application and perfection, depends on the work of the Holy Spirit.*

God the Father's glorious plan to save sinners and God the Son's death to redeem them would have been ineffective without the Spirit's work. It is the Holy Spirit alone who brings sinners from their pitiful, sinful condition to accept and enjoy salvation.

2. *The condition on which the Spirit would be given to the church has been fulfilled.*[4]

God made two great promises to sinners which include all that we need. One is that his Son would die for the elect. Secondly, God promised to give his Holy Spirit to work in them. Both promises are interrelated and inseparable, but the second promise depends on the first. Now that the first promise and condition has been met, then the second must be honoured (John 7:39; 16:7). Here is a powerful incentive to pray for the Holy Spirit (Luke 11:13).

3. *Another encouragement to expect revival is to consider that we live under the supervision of the Spirit, and in a period when the promises concerning him are being fulfilled.*[5]

The great blessing in the New Testament is the Holy Spirit. In the first outpouring of the Spirit (Acts 2) his supervision was established, and this will continue until the end of the gospel age. The age of the outpouring of the Spirit has not ceased.

4. *To strengthen our expectation of the Spirit, consider further the graciousness of this great blessing.*[6]

Rees reminds us that in Scripture there is a comparison between the 'pouring' out of the Spirit and water (Isaiah 49:10; 41:17-18; Titus 3:3-6 and John 7:37-39). And this great blessing of the Spirit is a sheer act of grace on God's part. Is not this the strongest encouragement for us to ask for, and expect, the Holy Spirit?

5. *Another consideration to strengthen our hope and longing expectation for the Holy Spirit is that he is promised in abundance and extensively to the church.*[7]

Rees emphasises that the word 'pour' in Acts 2:17, 33 indicates abundance (Titus 3:5-6; John 7:37-39), and the reference to 'all flesh' strengthens the idea but also points to the extensiveness of the Spirit's reception and ministry, including all ages and groups of people.

Effects of revival

For the rest of his sermon, Henry Rees highlights some of the effects of this outpouring of the Spirit. One effect is that there are many conversions, as in the Acts, and spiritual knowledge is given to all groups of people.[8] Other effects of genuine revival are: a greater degree of holiness in the church,[9] spiritual worship and effective use of the means of grace,[10] as well as peace and considerable success in the outward circumstances of the church.[11]

Persevering prayer

As he concludes his sermon, Rees exhorts Christians to persevere in prayer for the Spirit to be poured out on the church. This priceless blessing, he urges, must be sought with their whole heart.[12]

Thomas Charles's *Christian Instructor and Catechism* confirms this emphasis on the need for prayer. 'How does the Holy Spirit work in his people?' is question 171. The answer is three-fold: 'He works with *invincible* power' (2 Corinthians 10:4-5; Ephesians 1:19-20); 'He works *sovereignly* . . .' (John 3:8), and

'He works *freely* without anything in us to constrain him' (Psalm 51:12).

Do Christians have responsibilities in this context? Charles indicates that Christians must 'pray for the Holy Spirit'. Using Luke 11:13, he quotes the words of the Lord Jesus in order to emphasise the need for persevering prayer:

> If you then, being evil, know how to give good gifts to your children, how much more will your heavenly Father give the Holy Spirit to those who ask him!

And that is what our forefathers have done in Wales and elsewhere in the past, whether as individuals, or as churches like Capel y Nant and Beddgelert. Preachers too, such as John Elias, Henry Rees, Christmas Evans, John Jones and a multitude of others—all these men wrestled with God in prayer throughout their ministries. Here is the way forward for the church today, as in all generations.

Notes

Chapter 1: Revivals in Wales

1. Henry Hughes, *Hanes Diwygiadau Crefyddol Cymru* (Gwasg Genedlaethol Gymreig, 1906), p.249.
2. A helpful biography is provided by Arnold Dallimore, *George Whitefield* (Banner of Truth, Edinburgh), vol. 1 (1970), and vol. 2 (1980).
3. An interesting account of the conversion and work of John and Charles Wesley in the context of revival in England, Wales, Scotland, America, and the Moravians is: A. Skevington Wood, *The Inextinguishable Blaze* (Paternoster, 1960).
4. See, for example, Eifion Evans, *Daniel Rowland and the Great Evangelical Awakening in Wales* (Banner of Truth, Edinburgh, 1985). This is a valuable book.
5. See, for example, Richard Bennett, *The Early Life of Howell Harris*, translated from the Welsh by Gomer M. Roberts (Banner of Truth, London, 1962). Reprinted, with additional material, under the title, *Howell Harris and the Dawn of Revival* (Evangelical Press of Wales, Bridgend, 1987). The Welsh title was *Blynyddoedd Cyntaf Methodistiaeth* (Caernarfon, 1909).
6. J. C. Ryle, *Five Christian Leaders of the Eighteenth Century* (Banner of Truth, 1960).
7. Eifion Evans, *When He Is Come: The 1858–60 Revival in Wales* (Evangelical Movement of Wales, 1959), p.44. See also Eifion Evans, *Fire in the Thatch: The True Nature of Religious Revival* (Bryntirion Press, 1996), pp.186-225.
8. *When He Is Come*, p.97.
9. Eifion Evans, *The Welsh Revival of 1904* (Evangelical Movement of Wales, 1969), p.9. Later editions (1987 and 2004) include an index.
10. Ibid., p.146.
11. Foreword to Noel Gibbard's valuable book, *On the Wings of the Dove: The International Effects of the 1904–05 Revival* (Bryntirion Press, 2002), p.9.
12. Ibid.
13. Edward Thomas, *Yr Hanesydd Methodistaidd* (Hughes & Son, Wrexham, 1903), pp.107-9. See also, D. E. Jenkins: *The Rev. Thomas Charles of Bala*, vol. ii, ch. xxix, pp.88-119.
14. Thomas, p.107.

15. D. D. Williams, *Llawlyfr Hanes y Cyfundeb* (Literature Committee of Presbyterian Church of Wales, Caernarfon, n.d.), pp.147-8.

16. Edward Griffiths, *The Presbyterian Church of Wales Historical Handbook 1735–1905* (Hughes & Son, Wrexham, n.d.), p.131.

17. Thomas Rees, *Papers on Subjects Relating to Wales* (John Snow & Co., London, 1867), p.93.

18. Ibid., p.95.

19. Evans, *When He Is Come*, p.10.

20. William Williams, *Welsh Calvinistic Methodism: A Historical Sketch of the Presbyterian Church of Wales*, 3rd edition enlarged with introduction and notes by Gwyn Davies (Bryntirion Press, 1998), p.184.

21. Griffiths, p.129.

22. Thomas, p.109.

23. D. D. Williams, *Llawlyfr Hanes y Cyfundeb*, p.148.

24. D. G. Evans, *A History of Wales 1815–1906* (University of Wales Press, Cardiff, 1989), p.91.

25. Evans, *Fire in the Thatch*, p.181.

26. *Cyfrol Goffa Diwygiad 1904–05*, ed. Sidney Evans and Gomer M. Roberts (Llyfrfa'r Methodistiaid Calfinaidd, Caernarfon, 1954), p.17.

27. R. Tudur Jones, *Grym y Gair a Fflam y Ffydd: Ysgrifau ar Hanes Crefydd yng Nghymru*, ed. D. Densil Morgan (Prifysgol Cymru, Bangor, 1998), p.297.

28. Ibid., p.298.

29. Griffith Owen, *Cofiant Cadwaladr Owen, Dolwyddelan* (Hughes & Son, Wrexham, 1896), p.93.

Chapter 2: Life in Wales, social and religious

1. John Davies, *Hanes Cymru: A History of Wales in Welsh* (Penguin Books, London, 1992), p.307. David Williams estimates it at 480,000: *A History of Modern Wales* (John Murray & Co., London, 1950), p.195. For Gareth Evans, the estimated population is 489,000 in 1750 and 530,000 in 1780: *A History of Wales, 1815–1906* (University of Wales Press, Cardiff, 1989), p.1.

2. Williams, *A History of Modern Wales*, p.195.

3. Peter Mathias, *The First Industrial Nation: An Economic History of Britain 1700–1914*, 2nd edition, p.167.

4. Davies, *Hanes Cymru*, p.307.

5. Harry Hearder, *Europe in the Nineteenth Century: 1830–1880* (London, 1966), p.181.

6. A. H. Dodd, *A Short History of Wales: Welsh Life and Customs from Pre-historic Times to the Present Day* (B. T. Batsford Ltd., London, 1972), p.135.

7. They had established over 150 meeting houses between 1790 and 1810.

8. Dodd, *A Short History of Wales*, p.135.

9. Davies, *Hanes Cymru*, p.328.

10. Williams, *A History of Modern Wales*, p.154.

11. Evans, *A History of Wales, 1815–1906*, p.119.

12. Henry Hughes, *Diwygiadau Crefyddol Cymru*, pp.221-2. See also, *Methodistiaeth Cymru*, 1.342.

13. Hughes, *Diwygiadau Crefyddol Cymru*, p.224.

14. H. Jenkins, 'The New Enthusiasts', *The Remaking of Wales in the Eighteenth Century*, ed. Trevor Herbert & Gareth Elwyn Jones (University of Wales Press, Cardiff, 1988), p.47.

15. For further details of the societies in north Wales, see Gomer M. Roberts, *Hanes Methodistiaid Galfinaidd Cymru*, vol. 1 (Caernarfon, 1973), pp.447-8; Goronwy P. Owen, *Methodistiaeth Llŷn ac Eifionydd* (1978), pp.68-99.

16. *The Remaking of Wales in the Eighteenth Century*, ed. Trevor Herbert & Gareth Elwyn Jones, p.51.

17. A. H. Williams, *Efengyliaeth yng Nghymru, c.1840–1875* (Amgueddfa Werin Cymru, 1982), p.7.

18. Ibid., p.27.

19. The Act of Uniformity in 1662 involved the ejection of between 1500 and 2000 ministers from their parishes for refusing to accept unconditionally the newly revised Anglican Prayer Book. 'Nonconformity had been forced to become Dissent', Williston Walker, *A History of the Christian Church* (T. & T. Clark, Edinburgh, 1953), p.474. For details relating to Wales, see B. G. Owens, R. Tudur Jones, 'Anghydffurfwyr Cymru, 1660–1662', *Y Cofiadur* (1962).

20. R. T. Jenkins, *Hanes Cymru yn y Ddeunawfed Ganrif* (Gwasg Prifysgol Cymru, 1928), p.101.

21. Rees, *Papers on Subjects Relating to Wales*, p.74.

22. R. T. Jenkins, p.101, refers to David Peter's *Hanes Crefydd yng Nghymru, 1816*, where these statistics are given. The Baptist details are based on those provided by Titus Lewis.

23. Scottish Baptists originated in Scotland in the eighteenth century, when Robert Sandeman developed a sect which his father-in-law John Glas founded in 1725. They were governed locally by a plurality of unpaid elders; an educated ministry was anathema to them, and they refused to use full-time pastors. A theological distinctive of this group was that a mere intellectual assent to doctrines was adequate as a requirement for church membership and salvation.

24. This term refers to Scottish Baptists who followed their founder, Robert Sandeman, in emphasising the intellectual nature of faith. A number of Baptist preachers like Christmas Evans (for a period) and J. R. Jones of Ramoth in north Wales were influenced by Sandemanianism. A. H. Williams reminds us that, by the end of the eighteenth century, Baptists were becoming so evangelical and 'methodist' that it made J. R. Jones turn his back on his fellow Baptists and form a Scottish Baptist group of churches in Wales: see *Efengyliaeth yng Nghymru c.1840–1875*, pp.7-8.

25. They practise the baptism of believers by immersion, but more often than not their theology is Arminian in character.

26. Following Arminius (1560–1609), who reacted against Calvin's teaching on the sovereignty of God in salvation. Arminius taught that God's election was due to his foreknowledge of how sinners would respond to the gospel. Other beliefs of Arminius included the universal purpose of Christ's death for all sinners, thus making salvation available and possible for everyone; then the emphasis on man's ability to accept or reject the gospel as he wishes, so that the choice of the people to be saved was not in God's hand as Calvin taught. 'Remonstrants' (Protesters) is another name that is sometimes used to describe Arminians; this was based on a document called 'The Remonstrance' (or protest), which the followers of Arminius prepared in 1610 in order to clarify and propagate their distinctive views.

27. A liberal religious movement within Protestantism which denies orthodox doctrines like the infallibility of Scripture, the Holy Trinity, sin, and the substitutionary death of Jesus Christ for sinners. In 1995, there were 195 Unitarian churches in Great Britain.

28. Born on Christmas Day 1766 near Llandysul in Carmarthenshire.

29. A brief outline and assessment of Christmas Evans's life and ministry is provided by Sulwyn Jones in his article 'Christmas Evans', *Evangelical Magazine of Wales*, 25.1 (February–March 1986), pp.12-14. For those able to read Welsh, a detailed account of Evans's life and a helpful discussion of his theology and influence are provided by D. Densil Morgan in *Christmas Evans a'r Ymneilltuaeth Newydd* (Gwasg Gomer, 1991). See also Tim Shenton, *Christmas Evans: The Life and Times of the One-eyed Preacher of Wales* (Evangelical Press, 2001).

30. Jenkins, *Hanes Cymru yn y Ddeunawfed Ganrif*, p.101.

31. Dodd, *A Short History of Wales*, 133.

32. *The Remaking of Wales in the Eighteenth Century*, ed. Trevor Herbert and Gareth Elwyn Jones, p.47.

33. Edward Thomas, *Yr Hanesydd Methodistaidd* (Hughes & Son, Wrexham, 1903), pp.95-110.

34. Ibid., p.106.

35. Anthony Jones, *Welsh Chapels* (National Museum ofWales, 1984), p.7.
36. Evans, *A History of Wales, 1815–1906*, p.76.

Chapter 3: Beddgelert: preparing the way

1. Henry Hughes, *Hanes Diwygiadau Crefyddol Cymru,* p.250.
2. This is assumed in *Methodistiaeth Cymru*, vol. ii, p.199. The assumption is based on the fact that in 1771 Dafydd Morris preached throughout Arfon and Llŷn areas. He preached in all the places where there was regular preaching provision, but no mention is made of Beddgelert.
3. Owen, *Methodistiaeth Llŷn ac Eifionydd*, p.93.
4. Ibid., p.94.
5. Ibid., p.95.
6. Emyr Roberts and E. Wyn James, *Robert Roberts: Yr Angel o Glynnog* (Evangelical Library of Wales, 1976), p.10.
7. This is an approximate date; 1765 is also suggested: see 'Diwygiadau Beddgelert', *Y Llenor*, vol. 1 (1895), p.23.
8. These were voluntary schools originally established by Griffith Jones, Llanddowror. The schools circulated and had a strong biblical and evangelistic thrust in eighteenth-century Wales.
9. Robert Jones, Rhos-lan, *Drych yr Amseroedd*, ed. G. M. Ashton (University of Wales Press, 1958), p.125.
10. Ibid.
11. *Y Llenor*, vol. 1, p.22.
12. Joseph Evans, *Biographical Dictionary* (Caernarfon, 1907), p.30.
13. See, for example, *Methodistiaeth Cymru*, vol. ii, p.199.
14. Ibid., pp.199-200.
15. Ibid., p.201.
16. William Williams, *Welsh Calvinistic Methodism*, Introduction and notes by Gwyn Davies, 3rd edition (Bryntirion Press 1998), p.181.

Chapter 4: Capel y Nant: sowing the seed

1. See, for example, W. Gilbert Williams, 'Dechreuad a Chynnydd Methodistiaeth yn Sir Gaernarfon', *Journal of the Historical Society of the Presbyterian Church of Wales*, xxxvii.3 (October 1952), p.33.
2. Ibid., pp.33-4.
3. William Roberts, *Dau Can Mlynedd o Hynafiaeth a Chrefydd yn Ardal Nant, Nanhoron* (Llyfrfa'r Methodistiaid Calfinaidd, n.d.), p.9.
4. Owen, *Methodistiaeth Llŷn ac Eifionydd*, pp.18-24.
5. *Journal of the Historical Society of the Presbyterian Church of Wales*, xxxvii.3, pp.35-6.

6. Ibid., p.36.

7. Roberts, *Dau Can Mlynedd*, p.2.

8. One of the most distinguished estates and families in Llŷn centuries ago in terms of heredity, wealth and nobility. On the father's side, through Rhys ab Gryffydd ab Llewelyn Fychan ab Cynfrig, the Nanhoron family was descended from the medieval Hywel Dda ('the Good'), Rhodri Mawr ('the Great'), king of the whole of Wales. See *Enwogion Llŷn* (Cynyrchion Eisteddfod Sarn Mellteyrn, 1883), pp.18-21.

9. *Journal of the Historical Society of the Presbyterian Church of Wales*, xxxvii.3, p.37.

10. Owen, *Methodistiaeth Llŷn ac Eifionydd*, p.24.

11. Robert Jones, *Drych yr Amseroedd*, p.79.

12. See *Methodistiaeth Llŷn ac Eifionydd*, pp.85-7.

13. Different dates are given by historians. See, for example, *Dau Can Mlynedd*, which dates it as 1772. However, the actual sign on the roadside, only 300 yards away from the old building, reads: 'An eighteenth century dissenters meeting house, Capel Newydd, built 1769.'

14. *Dau Can Mlynedd*, p.35.

15. Ibid., p.25.

16. Ibid., p.16.

17. One of the earliest and legible inscriptions I could read clearly referred in Welsh to 'M. Williams, Talafan, aged 25, who died in 1824'.

18. William Roberts gives the date as 1772. See *Dau Can Mlynedd*, p.25.

19. *Dau Can Mlynedd*, p.26.

20. Ibid., p.25.

21. Quoted by Celia Lucas in 'Gardener on the high seas', *Liverpool Daily Post*, 19 August 1993, p.21. For a detailed history of Edwards's naval career, as well as his gardening interests in Nanhoron, see David Ellison, *Hammer and Nails* (Gwynedd Archives, 1994).

22. Harri Parri has written an interesting historical novel in Welsh on the conversion of Catherine Edwards, and her response, and the responses of others, to her conversion and involvement in the Nonconformist cause. See *Etholedig Arglwyddes* (Gwasg Pantycelyn, 1993).

23. *Dau Can Mlynedd*, p.45.

Chapter 5. Revival comes to Capel y Nant

1. While Thomas Charles probably knew of the first Sunday school established by Robert Raikes in Gloucester in 1780, Charles himself worked hard from 1787 to establish Sunday schools in Wales. This was a natural and successful development of Charles's work in establishing day schools in

needy areas for six to nine months, to teach children to read the Welsh Bible. See Welsh article, 'Ten reasons why I love to go to Sunday school', *Goleuad Cymru*, vol. IV, no. lxxix (May 1825), p.111. See also D. E. Jenkins, *The Life of the Rev. Thomas Charles of Bala*, in three volumes: vol. 1: 1755–1789; vol. 2: 1784–1805; vol. 3: 1804–1814 (Llewelyn Jenkins, Denbigh, 1908).

2. Henry Hughes, *Hanes Diwygiadau Crefyddol Cymru*, p.254.

3. Tudur Jones draws attention to only three of these catechisms: *The Catechism of Griffith Jones, Llanddowror*, 1743 (although the title was changed in 1749); *Catecism Gwŷr y Gymanfa* (The Catechism of the Assembly Men) and Thomas Charles's *Instructor*. Griffith Jones's Catechism was produced in the eighteenth century, but it continued its influence well into the nineteenth century when it was republished again in 1820. See R. Tudur Jones, *Grym y Gair a Fflam y Ffydd*, pp.270-7.

4. *Grym y Gair a Fflam y Ffydd*, p.271.

5. William Williams, *Welsh Calvinistic Methodism*, p.196.

6. Edward Griffiths, *The Presbyterian Church of Wales Historical Handbook 1735–1905* (Hughes & Son, Wrexham, n.d.), p.43.

7. *Catecism Byrraf Gwŷr y Gymanfa* (The Shorter Catechism of the Assembly Men).

8. Jones, *Grym y Gair a Fflam y Ffydd*, p.276.

9. See, for example, *Methodistiaeth Cymru*, vol. ii, pp.172-7.

10. *Y Drysorfa*, vol. xliv, no. 525 (July 1874), pp.246-7.

11. 30 September–1 October 1813.

12. *The Works of Jonathan Edwards*, vol. 2 (Banner of Truth, 1974), pp.278-312.

13. Ibid., p.283.

14. Ibid., p.282.

15. *Y Drysorfa* (July 1874), p.246.

16. Ibid.

17. *Methodistiaeth Cymru*, vol. ii, p.176.

18. William Roberts claims that this girl was the daughter of Hugh Williams, the Factory, who was an elder of the church at Capel y Nant and probably the man who introduced the *Instructor* and urged the church to pray daily for revival. This girl became a strong Christian and faithful church member. She eventually married and went to live with her husband in Murpoeth. See William Roberts, *Dau Can Mlynedd*, p.18.

19. *Methodistiaeth Cymru*, vol. ii, p.177.

Chapter 6: Revival approaches Beddgelert

1. 'Constitution and Church Government', *The History, Constitution, Rules of Discipline, and Confession of Faith . . . of the Calvinistic Methodists, or the*

    Presbyterians of Wales (published for the General Assembly by D. O'Brien Owen, Caernarfon, 1900), p.33.

2. Ibid., p.34.

3. *Y Llenor*, vol. 1 (1895), p.42.

4. John Jones, *Goleuad Cymru*, vol. III (1823), p.5.

5. Ibid., p.6.

6. Robert Ellis's chronology is unreliable. See, for example, Henry Hughes in his *Owen Owens, Cors-y-Wlad* (Dolgellau,1898), p.38; *Methodistiaeth Cymru,* vol. 1, pp.269-70 and vol. 2, 201-2. I am grateful to Geraint Jones, Cardiff, for stimulating me to reassess the chronology of these events.

7. Henry Hughes, *Hanes Diwygiadau Crefyddol Cymru*, p.260.

8. Ibid.

9. William Williams, *Welsh Calvinistic Methodism*, 3rd edition, enlarged (Bryntirion Press, 1998), p.182.

10. See 'Memorandum book of John Elias 1817–22', CMA Bala 56, National Library of Wales.

11. 'List of preachers at Tremadog 1813–37', CMA General Collection E106/2, National Library of Wales. Henry Hughes uses this evidence to discount the claim that Elias preached in Tremadog that same evening: *Hanes Diwygiadau Crefyddol Cymru*, pp.259-60. W. Hobley, *Hanes Methodistiaeth Arfon: Dosbarth Caernarfon, Ardaloedd Waunfawr a Beddgelert* (published by Arfon Monthly Meeting, MCMXIII), p.140, also accepts Hughes's evidence as being persuasive. However, William Williams is one of several writers who wrongly claims that Elias preached in Tremadog when Richard Williams was in Hafod y Llan. See *Welsh Calvinistic Methodism*, 3rd edition, p.182; cf. *Y Llenor*, vol. 1 (1895), p.44.

12. Hughes, *Hanes Diwygiadau Crefyddol Cymru*, p.263.

13. *Y Llenor*, vol. 1 (1895), p.44.

14. Jones, *Goleuad Cymru*, vol. III (1823), pp.5-9.

15. There is uncertainty regarding the precise text. Rev. Robert Ellis, who was present, is unsure whether it was Matthew 11:28 or John 6:44. See *Hanes Diwygiadau Crefyddol Cymru,* p.261.

16. The Authorised Version equivalent to the 1620 Welsh version used.

17. John Owen Jones, *Cofiant a Gweithiau y Parch Robert Ellis, Ysgoldy* (Caernarfon, 1883), pp.228-9.

18. Ibid.

19. Jones, *Goleuad Cymru*, vol. III (1823), p.6.

20. *Y Llenor*, vol. 1 (1895), p.44.

21. *Hanes Diwygiadau Crefyddol Cymru*, pp.262-3.

22. *Goleuad Cymru* (1823), p.6.
23. *Cofiant a Gweithiau y Parch Robert Ellis*, p.229.
24. Ibid.
25. *Y Llenor* (1895), p.44.
26. *Goleuad Cymru* (1823), p.6.
27. *Y Llenor* (1895), p.45.

Chapter 7: Revival reaches Beddgelert

1. Dr D. Martyn Lloyd-Jones in his Introduction to William Williams, *The Experience Meeting: An Introduction to the Welsh Societies of the Evangelical Awakening* (Bryntirion Press, 1973), p.5.
2. Ibid.
3. Robert Ellis claims that this *seiat* was held soon after, and not after the remarkable Sunday school incident later in September: see *Cofiant a Gweithiau y Parch Robert Ellis, Ysgoldy*, p.229. See also, W. Hobley, *Hanes Methodistiaeth Arfon: Dosbarth Caernarfon, Ardaloedd Waunfawr a Beddgelert* (published by Arfon Monthly Meeting, MCMXIII), pp.140-1, and *Diwygiadau Crefyddol Cymru*, p.263.
4. *Cofiant a Gweithiau y Parch Robert Ellis, Ysgoldy*, p.229.
5. Males numbered 356 and females 391. By the 1821 census the figure had increased to 436 males and 431 females, making a total of 867.
6. *Diwygiadau Crefyddol Cymru*, p.264.
7. Ibid.; cf. *Cofiant a Gweithiau y Parch Robert Ellis, Ysgoldy*, p.230.
8. See, for example, W. Hobley, *Methodistiaeth Arfon*, p.141.
9. Geraint Jones informs me that Henry Hughes's date of 21 September is probably confirmed in the *Dyddiadur Methodistiaid* for 1842 under 'Fairs of Wales'. Fair dates for Beddgelert are given as 10 April, 16 August and 21 September. The assumption is that the September date was the same in 1817.
10. *Thomas Charles' Spiritual Counsels: Selected from his Letters and Papers by Edward Morgan* (first published, 1836; Banner of Truth edition, 1993), p.433.
11. Ibid., p.434.
12. Ibid., p.435.
13. Ibid., pp.435-6.
14. Ibid., p.436.
15. It has been assumed for many years that Roberts quoted from the hymn of Pedr Fardd (1775–1845; he was Peter Jones, Liverpool), '*Dywedwyd ganwaith na chawn fyw . . .*' which is number 469 in *Llyfr Emynau y Methodistiaid Calfinaidd a Wesleaidd, 1927* (p.106). However, in a collection of essays by various authors (H. Elvet Lewis, G. Campbell Morgan, I.

V. Neprash) in *Glory Filled the Land: a Trilogy on the Welsh Revival 1904–1905*, ed. Richard O Roberts (International Awakening Press, Wheaton, Illinois, 1989), p.19, Elfed is probably correct when he writes: 'A line out of one of Williams of Pantycelyn's hymns seemed to possess him, "God's grasp is surest"; and as he repeated it more than once, the feeling which had melted and awed the young women's class affected the whole school.'

The hymn by Pantycelyn to which Elfed refers is number 101 in the same hymn book and begins with the words, '*Ti, Iesu, ydwyt oll dy Hun, / Fy meddiant ar y llawr.*' However, it is only in the last line of the very last verse that the words quoted by Richard Roberts appear.

Geraint Jones informs me that, according to *Emynau a'u Hawduriaid* by John Thickens and Gomer Roberts, the hymn by Pedr Fardd ('*Dywedwyd ganwaith . . .*'), with fifteen verses, each ending with '*Mae'r afael sicraffry*' did not appear until the June 1838 edition of *Yr Athraw*. It seems more probable, therefore, that Richard Roberts was quoting from the earlier hymn written by Pantycelyn.

16. *Cofiant a Gweithiau y Parch Robert Ellis, Ysgoldy*, p.227; quoted also in *Y Drysorfa*, vol. xlviii, p.379.

Chapter 8: Revival power and heavenly singing

1. *Y Llenor*, vol. 1 (1895), p.45.
2. *Drych yr Amseroedd*, p.125.
3. Ibid., pp.125-6.
4. *Cofiant a Gweithiau y Parch Robert Ellis, Ysgoldy*, p.231.
5. Ibid., p.230.
6. *Y Llenor* (1895), p.45.
7. *Diwygiadau Crefyddol Cymru*, pp.259-60. See also, for example, *Y Llenor* (1895), pp.47-8.
8. Geraint Jones has searched John Elias's memorandum books (CMA Bala 56, NLW) for the period 1817–1822 and confirms that the last Sunday in November 1817 was the only Sunday that John Elias preached at Tremadog; he also preached in Beddgelert the previous Saturday evening. Was it over the last weekend in November 1817 that the incident of this group not going to Tremadog as planned occurred? We cannot be dogmatic. I concur with Geraint Jones, however, that D. E. Jenkins (*Beddgelert: Its Facts, Fairies and Folklore*, pp.367-9) is unjustified in claiming that the events occurred in 1820, especially as John Jones, Nanmor, says: 'this remarkable service was about the time of the beginning of "the Great Revival".' (See also notes 10 and 11 on p.182.)

9. *Diwygiadau Crefyddol Cymru*, p.260.
10. See manuscript 'John Jones, Nanmor', in National Library of Wales, CMA General 8661.
11. *Y Llenor*, vol. 1 (1895), p.49.
12. Ibid., p.50.
13. Ibid., p.48.
14. Ibid., p.49.
15. In Welsh it is described as 'y canu yn yr awyr', literally, 'the singing in the air'.
16. *Methodistiaeth Cymru*, vol. 1, pp.270-1.
17. Ibid.
18. Ibid., p.272.
19. Ibid., p.273.
20. Ibid.
21. Quite close geographically to the places mentioned in this chapter is Egryn, near Harlech. Here, in the 1904 Revival, a housewife, Mrs Mary Jones, had unbounded evangelistic zeal and was greatly used by the Lord. Eifion Evans reports: 'On the way to the church she would see lights in the sky in the form of a pillar of fire, a claim which was substantiated by several independent witnesses.' These were received by her as particular guidance regarding her visiting and the number of converts to be expected in a meeting. See Eifion Evans, *The Welsh Revival of 1904* (Bryntirion Press, 1969), pp.115-16.

Chapter 9: Preaching: its importance

1. *Confession of Faith of the Calvinistic Methodists, 1823* (English translation published for the General Assembly in 1900, Caernarfon), p.41.
2. Ibid., p.39.
3. Ibid., p.54.
4. Ibid., p.56.
5. Ibid., pp.56-7.
6. Ibid., p.75.
7. Edward Morgan, *John Elias, His Life and Letters* (Banner of Truth, 1973), p.349.
8. *Confession of Faith*, p.80.
9. Ibid., p. 80.
10. Ibid., p.80.
11. Ibid., p.79.
12. Ibid., p.79.

13. Ibid., pp.54-5.
14. Ibid., p.110.
15. Ibid., p.88.
16. Ibid., p.81.
17. Ibid., p.107.
18. R. Tudur Jones, *John Elias: Prince Amongst Preachers* (Evangelical Library of Wales, 1975), p.22.
19. Ibid., p.23. For a summary of the sermon, see also, Edward Morgan: *John Elias: Life and Letters* (Banner of Truth, 1973), pp.406-8.
20. Jones, *John Elias*, 23.
21. Edward Griffiths, *The Presbyterian Church of Wales Historical Handbook, 1735–1905* (Hughes & Son, Wrexham, n.d.).
22. Ibid., p.49.
23. Ibid., p.50.
24. Ibid., p.49.
25. Ibid., pp.86-107.
26. Ibid., p.86.
27. Edward Parry, *Llawlyfr ar Hanes* y *Diwygiadau Crefyddol yng Nghymru* (Corwen, 1898), p.107.

Chapter 10: Powerful preaching

1. Quoted by Emyr Roberts in *Robert Roberts: Yr Angel o Glynnog* by Emyr Roberts and E. Wyn James (Evangelical Library of Wales, 1976), p.5.
2. Owen Thomas, *Cofiant John Jones, Talsarn* (Wrexham, 1874), p.806.
3. *Diwygiadau Crefyddol Cymru*, p.227.
4. D. Densil Morgan, *Christmas Evans a'r Ymneilltuaeth Newydd* (Gwasg Gomer, Llandysul, 1991), p.22.
5. Ibid., pp.50-1.
6. Ibid., p.71.
7. Eifion Evans, *Fire in the Thatch*, p.184.
8. Ibid., p.185.
9. William Williams, *Welsh Calvinistic Methodism*, 3rd edition, p.253.
10. Ibid., p.254.
11. *Y Llenor*, vol. 1 (1895).
12. *Goleuad Cymru*, vol. III (1822), pp.5-9.
13. Ibid., p.9.
14. Ibid., p.8.
15. *Y Llenor*, vol. I (1895), p.50.

16. Ibid.
17. *Goleuad Cymru*, vol. III (1822), p.7.
18. Ibid.
19. Ibid.
20. Ibid.

Chapter 11: Association preaching during revival

1. J. Morgan Jones and William Morgan, *Y Tadau Methodistaidd*, vol. 2 (1897), p.338.
2. Ibid., p.339. It is uncertain if the preacher was named Dafydd William Rhys or Dafydd Williams.
3. The Welsh word is '*seiat*'.
4. *Y Tadau Methodistaidd*, vol. 2, p.340.
5. Ibid., p.352.
6. *Cymru*, vol. XIX (1900), p.25.
7. *The History, Constitution, Rules of Discipline and Confession of Faith of the Calvinistic Methodists, 1823*, English Version published for the General Assembly by D. O'Brien Owen (The Bookroom, Caernarfon, 1900), p.36.
8. Ibid.
9. Ibid.
10. J. O. Jones, *Cofiant a Gweithiau y Parch. Robert Ellis, Ysgoldy* (Caernarfon, 1883), p.233.
11. Ibid., p.234.
12. Ibid.
13. Ibid.
14. *Y Tadau Methodistaidd*, vol. 2, p.350; taken from *Cofiant John Jones, Talsarn*, p.842.
15. The full account is provided in O. Jones, *Some of the Great Preachers of Wales* (reprinted by Tentmaker Publications, 1995), pp.234-40.
16. *Crynodeb o Dair o Bregethau a bregethwyd yn Nghymanfaoedd y Bala, gan y diweddar Barch. Ebenezer Morris* (Clwyd-Wasg, Denbigh, 1825).
17. Ibid., pp.10-12.
18. *Y Tadau Methodistaidd*, vol. 2, p.354.
19. I am using parts of Jones's summary.
20. D. Jones, *Crynodeb o Dair o Bregethau*, p.7.
21. *Y Tadau Methodistaidd*, vol. 2, p.355.
22. Edward Griffiths, *The Presbyterian Church of Wales Historical Handbook 1735–1905* (Wrexham, n.d.), p.59.

Chapter 12: Dolwyddelan: the dawn before revival

1. Owen Thomas, *Cofiant John Jones, Talsarn, Gyda Hanes Duwinyddiaeth a Phregethu Cymru* (Hughes & Son, Wrexham, 1874), p.24.
2. Griffith Owen, *Cofiant y Parch. Cadwaladr Owen, Dolwyddelan* (Wrexham, 1896), p.19.
3. Ibid., p.48.
4. Ibid., p.57.
5. Ibid., p.74.
6. T. Rees and J. Thomas, *Hanes Eglwysi Annibynol Cymru*, vol. 3 (Liverpool, 1873), p.310.
7. Ibid., p.311.
8. See, for example, *Hanes Eglwysi Annibynol Cymru*, vol. 3, footnote on pp.310-11; *Diwygiadau Crefyddol Cymru*, pp.280-2.
9. D. Charles Evans, *Adgofion am y Diweddar Barchedig David Jones, Treborth* (Dolgellau, 1886), p.41; see also pp.26-8, 39-44.
10. Ibid., pp.39-44.
11. Ibid.
12. Ibid.

Chapter 13: Dolwyddelan in revival

1. D. Charles Evans, *Adgofion am y Diweddar Barchedig David Jones, Treborth*, pp.39-44.
2. Ibid., p.26.
3. Ibid.
4. Ibid., pp.39-44.
5. Ibid.
6. Ibid., pp.26-7.
7. Owen Thomas, *Cofiant John Jones, Talsarn*, pp.55-6.
8. Ibid., p.56.
9. Ibid., p.62.
10. Ibid., pp.59-60.
11. Ibid., pp.62-3.
12. Ibid., pp.68-9.
13. Ibid., p.69.

Chapter 14: Revival phenomena

1. Appendix A, 'William Williams and Welsh Calvinistic Methodism', in William Williams, *Welsh Calvinistic Methodism*, 3rd edition (Bryntirion Press, 1998), p.279.

2. 'Barn Bersonol', *Seren Cymru*, 10 April 1998, p.7.
3. *Welsh Calvinistic Methodism*, 3rd edition, p.14.
4. Ibid., p.186.
5. Ibid., p.187.
6. Ibid.
7. Ibid., p.188.
8. Eifion Evans, *Pursued by God: A Selective Translation, with Notes, of the Welsh Religious Classic 'Theomemphus' by William Williams of Pantycelyn* (Bryntirion Press, 1996), p.13.
9. Ibid.
10. Ibid., 'blurb' on back cover.
11. Ibid., pp.50-1.
12. Ibid., p.53.
13. Ibid., p.183.
14. Emyr Roberts and R. Geraint Gruffydd, *Revival and Its Fruit* (Evangelical Library of Wales, Bridgend, 1981), p.25.
15. Ibid., p.27.
16. This translation is provided by R. Geraint Gruffydd on p.27.
17. *Revival and Its Fruit*, p.29.
18. Ibid., p.30.
19. Ibid., pp.31-2.
20. 254/1; quoted and translated by Eifion Evans in *Pursued by God*, p.183.
21. Quoted by Eifion Evans in *Fire in the Thatch* (Bryntirion Press, 1996), pp.14-15. See also, William Williams, *The Experience Meeting—An Introduction to the Welsh Societies of the Evangelical Awakening*, translated by Bethan Lloyd-Jones (Evangelical Movement of Wales, 1973), pp.8-9,11.
22. *Pursued by God*, p.184.

Chapter 15: Revival impacts north Wales

1. Eifion Evans, *Fire in the Thatch*, p.184.
2. *Adgofion David Jones*, p.27.
3. Eifion Evans, *When He Is Come*, 2nd edition (Evangelical Movement of Wales, 1967), pp.115, 119.
4. Ibid., pp.109-10.
5. *Welsh Calvinistic Methodism*, 3rd edition, pp.184-5.
6. Ibid., p.185.
7. *Llawlyfr ar Hanes y Diwygiadau Crefyddol yng Nghymru*, p.106.
8. Thomas, *Yr Hanesydd Methodistaidd* (Wrexham, 1903), p.109.

9. *Fire in the Thatch*, p.181.
10. *Welsh Calvinistic Methodism*, 3rd edition, p.185.
11. Griffith Parry, *Cofiant a Gweithiau Y Parch. Robert Owen, Llundain* (Manchester, 1880), p.21.
12. Ibid.
13. 'Dechreuad a Chynnydd Methodistiaeth yn Sir Gaernarfon', in *Journal of the Historical Society of the Presbyterian Church of Wales*, xxxvii.3 (October 1952), p.43.
14. Edward Morgan, *John Elias: Life and Letters* (Banner of Truth, 1973), p.16.
15. Ibid., p.17.
16. *Cofiant a Gweithiau y Parch. Robert Owen*, p.22.
17. Ibid., p.24.

Chapter 16: 'Keeping the fire going'

1. J. M. Jones and W. Morgan, *Y Tadau Methodistaidd*, vol. 2 (Swansea, 1897), p.357.
2. Ibid.
3. Joseph Evans, *Biographical Dictionary* (Caernarfon, 1907), p.226.
4. See Chapter 10 for more details.
5. Evans, *Biographical Dictionary*, p.256.
6. 'Gomer M. Roberts', *The Dictionary of Welsh Biography Down to 1940* , ed. J. E. Lloyd and R. T. Jenkins (London, 1959), p.848.
7. Chapter 3.
8. Evans, *Biographical Dictionary*, p.264.
9. Ibid., p.16; for more details see Eifion Evans, *Daniel Rowland and the Great Evangelical Awakening in Wales* (Banner of Truth, 1985), pp.331-3.
10. D. E. Jenkins, *The Life of the Rev. Thomas Charles B.A. of Bala*, vol. 1 (1908), pp.35, 173, 542.
11. Evans, *Biographical Dictionary*, p.20.
12. Iain Murray, *Thomas Charles' Spiritual Counsel* (Banner of Truth, 1993), p.xxvi.
13. *Atgofion John Evans y Bala*, p.22.
14. Ibid., p.23.
15. Goronwy P. Owen, *Methodistiaeth Llŷn ac Eifionydd*, p.105.
16. *The Dictionary of Welsh Biography Down to 1940*, pp.507-8.
17. *A Light in the Land: Christianity in Wales 200–2000 AD* (Bryntirion Press, 2002), p.87.

18. 'Idwal Jones', *The Dictionary of Welsh Biography Down to 1940*, p.516.
19. *Cofiant Thomas Jones o Ddinbych*, ed. Humphreys and Roberts (1820); reprinted, ed. Idwal Jones (Gwasg Aberystwyth, 1937).
20. For further details, see, for example, Tim Shenton, *Christmas Evans: Life and Times of the One-eyed Preacher of Wales* (Evangelical Press, Darlington, 2001), pp.238-43.

Chapter 17: A fruit of revival: preachers

1. See Chapters 3 and 10 for more details.
2. *Methodistiaeth Llŷn ac Eifionydd*, p.188.
3. Ibid., p.189.
4. Ibid.
5. John Jones, *Cofiant y Parch. Michael Roberts, Pwllheli* (1883), p.73. I have given a fuller description of the Pennant service in Chapter 15.
6. *Adgofion Hiraethog am y Parch. Michael Roberts, Pwllheli* (Liverpool, 1903), pp.45-6.
7. Ibid., pp.46-7.
8. Referred to earlier in Chapter 13.
9. John Jones, *Cofiant y Parch. Michael Roberts, Pwllheli*, p.75.
10. Ibid., p.109.
11. *Methodistiaeth Llŷn ac Eifionydd*, p.189.
12. R. Tudur Jones, *John Elias: Prince Amongst Preachers* (Evangelical Library of Wales, 1975).
13. Ibid., p.4.
14. Ibid., pp.32-3.
15. R. Tudur Jones, *Grym y Gair a Fflam y Ffydd*, p.298.
16. Ibid., p.182.
17. Griffith Owen, *Cofiant Cadwaladr Owen* (Wrexham, 1896).
18. See, for example, the varying quality of his sermons in the two volumes: D. Griffith, *Cyfrol Cynta o Bregethau gan y Barch. W. Rees* (Denbigh, 1881); D. Griffith, *Ail Gyfrol o Bregethau gan y Barch. W. Rees* (Denbigh, 1910). Also consult 'Gwilym Hiraethog (1802–1883)' in *Grym y Gair a Fflam y Ffydd*, pp.183-93.
19. Edward Griffiths, *The Presbyterian Church of Wales Historical Handbook 1735–1905* (Wrexham, n.d.), p.67.
20. There are three volumes of his sermons published: *Pregethau Gan y Diweddar Barchedig Henry Rees*, vol. 1 (Caernarfon, 1872); *Pregethau Gan y Diweddar Barchedig Henry Rees*, vol. 2 (Holywell, 1875); *Pregethau Gan y Diweddar Barchedig Henry Rees*, vol. 3 (Holywell, 1881). See also

'Pregethau Henry Rees (1798–1865) a Gwilym Hiraethog' in *Grym y Gair a Fflam y Ffydd*, pp.194-209.

21. *Cofiant a Gweithiau y Parch. Robert Owen, Llundain*, p.25.

Chapter 18: The way forward today

1.   Edward Morgan, *John Elias: Life and Letters* (Banner of Truth, 1973), p.228.

2.   Ibid.

3.   *Pregethau Henry Rees*, vol. 1 (Caernarfon, 1872), p.409.

4.   Ibid. pp.411-12.

5.   Ibid., pp.412-13.

6.   Ibid., pp.414-16.

7.   Ibid., pp.416-20.

8.   Ibid., p.422.

9.   Ibid., p.423.

10. Ibid., p.425.

11. Ibid., pp.426-7.

12. Ibid., p.429.

Index

COMMENDATIONS

'Eryl Davies has given us a thoroughly researched account of the often quoted but little understood revival at Capel y Nant and Beddgelert from 1817 to 1822, but it is far more than this: the assessment of eighteenth- and nineteenth-century revivals in north Wales, together with the individual cameos, provide us with the heartbeat of true spiritual revival—a book for all who have a longing for God to honour his name.'

Brian Edwards
Author of *Revival—a people saturated with God* and other titles

'Eryl Davies's meticulous account of the divine visitation in and around rural Beddgelert between 1817 and 1822 informs the mind, warms the heart, and prompts prayer for similar touches of God today.'

J. I. Packer
Author of *Knowing God* and many other titles

'The half-century between 1790 and 1840 was a time of significant spiritual and cultural renewal in Wales. Indeed, it has been aptly described as the 'Second Evangelical Awakening'. Of pivotal importance was the powerful 'Beddgelert Revival' of 1817–22, which had a major impact not only on church life, but also on political, social and cultural life in general. Despite its importance, this revival has received rather scant attention. Dr Eryl Davies is to be warmly commended, therefore, for providing this in-depth study of a key period in the formation of modern Wales.'

E. Wyn James
School of Welsh, Cardiff University

'We are greatly indebted to Dr Eryl Davies for this thorough work of research. It should encourage a serious study of other neglected revivals. It also provides valuable insights into the nature of revival—something that is much needed in the present church situation. Furthermore, it should stimulate prayerful concern for revival in our day.'

Noel Gibbard
Author of *On the Wings of the Dove* and other Welsh Revival titles